My Debt to You

My Debt to You

by Elvage G. Murphy

My Debt to You

Copyright © 2022 Elvage G. Murphy, J.D.
All rights reserved.

No part of this publication may be reproduced, stored in a retrieval system or transmitted in any way by any means, electronic, mechanical, photocopy, recording or otherwise without the prior permission of the author except as provided by USA copyright law.

The opinions expressed by the author are not necessarily those of Wisdom House Books, Inc.

Published by Wisdom House Books, Inc.
Chapel Hill, North Carolina 27516 USA
1.919.914.6299 | www.wisdomhousebooks.com

Wisdom House Books is committed to excellence in the publishing industry.
Book design copyright © 2022 by Wisdom House Books, Inc. All rights reserved.
Cover and Interior Design by Ted Ruybal
Published in the United States of America

Paperback ISBN: 978-0-578-93982-7
LCCN: 2021916364

1. BIO 002010 | Biography and Autobiography / Cultural, Ethnic and Regional / African-American and Black
2. EDU 022000 | Parent Participation
3. FAM 037000 | Family and Relationships / Prejudice
4. SOC 031000 | Discrimination
5. SOC 070000 | Race and Ethnic Relations

First Edition

25 24 23 22 21 20 / 10 9 8 7 6 5 4 3 2 1

Table of Contents

Introduction: My Debt to You vii

Chapter I: It Is What It Is. 1

Chapter II: America's Measuring Stick 7

Chapter III: Becoming Equipped 13

Chapter IV: Something's Not Right 25

Chapter V: The Rules Are Different for Us 39

Chapter VI: Do Not Submit to Fear 47

Chapter VII: The Fight for Justice Is a Partnership. 57

Chapter VIII: All They See Is This. 67

Chapter IX: It's Not Personal. 75

Chapter X: Own It 83

Chapter XI: Our Posterity 89

Chapter XII: I Have a Purpose. 93

Chapter XIII: My Hood: A Lesson in Diversity and Inclusion 109

Chapter XIV: The Fulfillment of a Mother's Vision and a Father's Passion . . . 123

Chapter XV: Conclusion: My Letters to America. 139

About the Author: 143

This memoir is dedicated to
my supportive spouse, partner
and best friend,

Dawn Janel Murphy

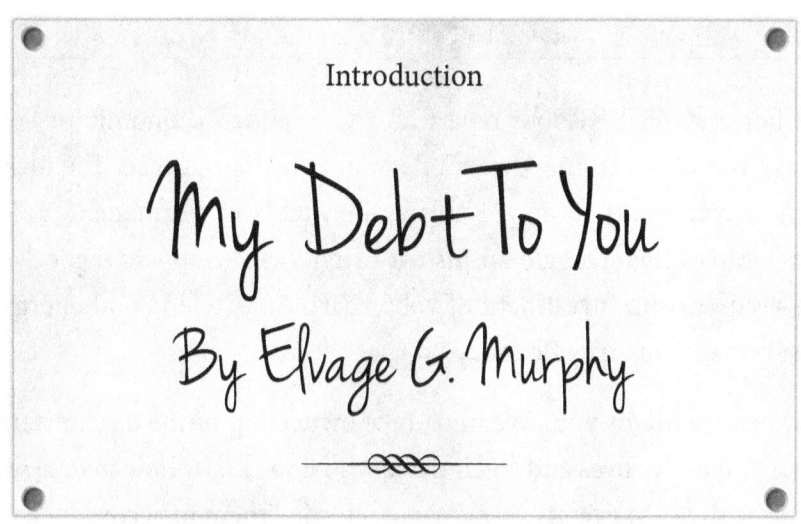

Introduction

My Debt To You

By Elvage G. Murphy

Dear Dr. King:

As a young boy, my mother and father encouraged my brother, Terrance, and I to listen to, read, and heed your words. Every time I did, the purpose for my life, although not clear, became evident to me; *I knew I had one*. Despite my academic and personal struggles, foolishness, and embarrassing moments, I never forgot your selfless dedication and commitment to the principles of freedom, equality, and justice. Your courage and sacrifices were extraordinary. The mistreatment and abuse you and your family endured is beyond my comprehension. Through it all, I now reap the benefit of a gift: *the gift of endless opportunity*. Because of you, I unequivocally know I can encounter hardship, bigotry, and policies designed to bar my progress and advancement, yet remain resolute in the pursuit of my passions and commitment to honor you and others who paved a road previously laid with legal and illegal obstacles, with a renewed paradigm of strength, commitment, and determination.

In my mind, the law and justice are inextricably linked. You showed me one cannot exist without the other. The law should and must establish the moral boundaries of a society. Justice ensures the law is equitably and fairly applied without regard to race, gender, economic or social status. The realist in me knows this is not always the case. The idealist in me never wants to accept this as inevitable or permanent. Taking ownership of this struggle for justice—right over wrong, and good over evil—required an investment of your heart, time, talent, and energy; it must remain our struggle today.

How can we honor you? We must take ownership of the circumstances in our respective lives and teach those who don't know how to take ownership of theirs to exercise every right afforded them in accordance with natural law. An extreme change of our people's paradigm has become necessary to assure our survival and prosperity. In order to fight for our dreams, we must be equipped to do battle. According to our brother, Booker T. Washington, *"No one should seek to close his eyes to the truth that the [African American people in the United States] is passing through a very serious and trying period of its development [and progress], a period that calls for the use of our ripest thought."*

Very simply, we must reverse the negative thinking that has allowed so many of us to excuse and celebrate underachievement and even failure, rather than simply making resolutions to reject negative and destructive influences in our lives. Taking responsibility or ownership of the issues within our community provides freedom to create our own lives; we must become empowered. Unless we recognize this truth, and use this power to transform ourselves, Dr. King, your efforts and the efforts of so many other Americans will be in vain.

It should be our privilege and blessing to honor your sacrifice. The history and legacy of the African American people is full of grand achievements. For the price you paid, my debt to you is to remain true to the strength and credibility of your legacy, achievements, and the pursuit for justice. It is the least I can do.

Chapter I

It is what it is

On November 7, 2017, I received a text message from a friend. The text referenced a link to *USA Today's* publication of findings identifying the five worst cities for black Americans. The number one ranked city served as the venue for my family's home, education, career, and community service activities for nearly twenty-three years: "24/7 Wall St. created an index on disparities[1] in . . . cit[ies] between black and white residents in various socioeconomic measures."[2] The publication concludes, "Despite the achievements of the Civil Rights Movement more than five decades ago, there exist substantial inequalities along racial lines in America."[3] Additionally, the report concluded, "Discriminatory policy, racial bias, and a history of oppression have widened the gap among black and white residents in a variety of socioeconomic measures."[4] In short, Erie,

---

1. Income, educational attainment, homeownership, poverty, unemployment, incarceration and mortality rates

2. https://247wallst.com/special-report/2017/11/03/thew-worst-cities-for-black-americans-2

3. Id.

4. Id.

Pennsylvania was at the top of the list. As I shared the news of this report with family, friends, and colleagues, many were not surprised. The responses were, "I knew I wasn't crazy," and "Finally! The world knows the truth." Some citizens were embarrassed. Some refused to accept the findings and were dismissive of its accuracy based on their knowledge or familiarity with the black people with whom they worked, or who lived in their neighborhoods. Often, this familiarity would be accompanied by the obvious question and remarks that pertained to me: "What about Elvage? He does well. See, black people do well in Erie." The exception to which they may be most familiar is belied by the reality of black people in Erie. Many citizens in the city of Erie were hopeful that such a revelation would finally bring much needed attention to the history of racial bias and discrimination which ails this city and widens the socioeconomic gulf that continues to exist between its citizens. I am certain some of Erie's citizens were not fazed by the findings, and others did not care. Most citizens resorted to the comfort of clinging to a familiar nostalgia of the Erie they remember from their childhood. Elected leaders of Erie have traditionally ignored or downplayed such revelations and avoid making any comment whatsoever for fear it will jeopardize their personal, or professional interests. In backroom offices, located down a corridor in government and office buildings, or private clubs, leaders concoct schemes designed to avoid giving acknowledgement to such findings. In time, the anger, embarrassment, and attention associated with such publicity passes. People go back to work, their children return to school, and attitudes remain the same.

After reviewing the 24/7 Wall Street article, I reflected on my family's experiences in Erie. By all accounts, it would not be a reach to state that our family prospered in Erie. We did not achieve the standards of success most attribute to the accumulation of wealth or notoriety. Something different defined and set our family apart. I can remember how often neighbors, friends, and colleagues would remark about the quality of my marriage to my wife, Janel, and the way we raised our children. We became viewed as a template or example to others.

The publication of these findings reminded me of the time when our family moved to Erie in August of 1995. I met people who would ask me, "You aren't from here, are you?" I would ask, "How can you tell?" They would say, "You don't act like someone from Erie." I had no idea how people from Erie acted. I am still not sure I do now. For the next ten years, I recalled being repeatedly asked the question, "Why are you here? You seem like you should be somewhere else like Atlanta or Washington, D.C." I would laugh it off and ask, "What is wrong with being in Erie?" Admittedly, I preferred to be elsewhere. Nevertheless, it was apparent that Erie would be a place my family and I would call home for over twenty-three years.

Our transition to Erie did not come without challenges. Like most communities its size, it is subject to a politically stagnant culture that embraces familiarity and comfort over talent and outsiders. Elected leaders struggle to cultivate a community in which all citizens can be assured of being valued and treated with respect and dignity. A high degree of mistrust and suspicion infuses its people. People who have lived in Erie their entire lives describe the city with acute nostalgia. Others who have moved away and return describe it as old-fashioned and behind the times. I have traveled to, and throughout, all of the southern states in America. Erie is the only place where I still hear white and black people commonly refer to African Americans as "colored" or "the coloreds." Erieites[5], as they often refer to themselves, seek to maintain their local flavor and outlook. Erieites yield to provincial characteristics and familiarity. Generation after generation of families are prone to live in the same neighborhoods, school districts, attend the same schools, and engage in celebratory activities that highlight their identities and traditions, etc. However, Erie was, and remains, a place where new people, initiatives, and perspectives are not well received. Those who are interested in maintaining the status quo receive new and innovative ideas with skepticism, doubt, and annoyance.

Erie was a tough town to navigate, and it was considered impenetrable if you were not willing to play by certain rules; and I was not. It is not for the faint of heart. Nevertheless, I was prepared to live and work there. I believed God grants us all the grace to transcend our circumstances. My grace happened to be in the form of a father and mother, and the examples they set for me. I learned from their successes and failures. Each and every lesson prepared me for the season of Erie that awaited me and my family. This book is in honor of a father and mother who gave everything they had and held nothing back to teach and prepare me to effectively negotiate the challenges of being black, the additional responsibilities and burdens we must carry and overcome, while being expected to honor the values and patriotism associated with being an American. It is my hope that black people will retake ownership of our lives and the lives of our children and commit to prepare them as my parents prepared their children for the reality of a hard, cruel world. It is my hope that white people will begin to appreciate and acknowledge that the black experience is not equivalent to their own, and that they

---

5. A term used by citizens of Erie use to identify their place of origin

will begin to inspire a change in the narrative in our country that is devoid of careless judgments and destructive language so that we may truly conform to the values we purport to represent. In short, America, you are being called into account.

Chapter II

America's Measuring Stick

The *Preamble to the United States Constitution* expresses the highest regard for unity. It calls for the pursuit of perfection, justice, peace, the protection and prosperity for our citizens, and to secure the blessings of freedom for future generations. Every part of this mandate implicitly calls for a spirit of excellence that can only be derived from our unequivocal allegiance to truth. In the United States, we have become diverted from this assignment. Like most mandates, it has the potential to interfere and upset what we consider to be of comfort to us.

In August of 2017, while teaching a course in *Race, Gender and Law* at my former university, I attempted to facilitate a discussion on the United States Constitution. I asked, "How many of you have read the United States Constitution?" None acknowledged they had. Then, I asked, "How many of you know the *Preamble to the United States Constitution*?" Some acknowledged reading it, and fewer remember having to recite it. After I advised my students that they owed it to themselves to know what is in the document that established the framework for our federal government and its relationship with our country's citizens, they were assigned to read and recite the *Preamble to the United States Constitution*. I also asked students to identify and explain what portions of the *Preamble* they believe best reflected the *vision, values, and mission statements* of the United States, and whether they believe they are living up to its mandate. They were also required to provide a well-reasoned explanation in support of their responses. Although the assignment was for a grade, I thought it was important for these seventeen- and eighteen-year-old students to give considerable thought to how they would internalize the words and phrases within the *Preamble*. Approximately a week later, each student was required to recite the *Preamble* before me. After managing their nerves and emotions, each student offered their recitation. What became a revelation to me was how much students revealed they did not know before reading and memorizing it, and how much they now understand they have a responsibility to carry this mandate forward. One assignment, worth twenty-five points, became an epiphany to not only thirty-two first-year students; it became an epiphany to me. I decided to look at the *Preamble* introspectively to measure myself against the expectations and mandates of its words. In short, I realized I have not always lived up to its mandate. According to Erwin Chemerinsky, ". . . [T]he Preamble states basic values that should guide the understanding of the Constitution."[1] From the perspectives of a lawyer and educator, I have read, taught, cited, and argued points of law related to the interpretation of the United States Constitution more times than I can remember. I also memorized and recited the words of the *Preamble* in the fourth grade, and I have never forgotten them. At this stage of my life, and considering the

---

1. Chemerinsky, Erwin, Giving meaning to the Preamble. Matters of Debate, National Constitution Center

crossroad at which our nation's families stand, I realized I owed it to my posterity to read it and "break it down" for my appreciation and personal edification so I can effectively fulfill my duty of citizenship. Each phrase and sentence has new meaning for me now.

> We the People of the United States, in order to form a more perfect union, establish justice, insure domestic tranquility, provide for the common defense, promote the general welfare, and secure the blessings of liberty to ourselves and our posterity, do ordain and establish this Constitution for the United States of America.
>
> —*Preamble to the United States Constitution*

The language of our nation's *Preamble* is clear. It is not confusing, and it is not necessary for our appreciation and understanding to subject it to critical analysis by the United States Supreme Court. First, the word "[W]e" denotes a call for unity, a collective purpose for a group of people. It does not call for the segregation and the superiority of one human being above another. The phrase "We the People of the United States" clearly defines to whom the preamble applies. "[I]n order to form a more perfect union," asserts all citizens of this country have the burden and responsibility to strive to form a nation that is entirely without fault or defect, while corresponding to an ideal standard in substance and representation. Our nation has a call to perfection! We are to strive to create a single unit or operate with a unified condition for a common purpose through the combining or coalition of different people with different opinions. The mission of the *Preamble* is to establish justice and peace at home, establish a defense capable of protecting its citizens, contribute to the growth or prosperity of our citizens' well being, and protect the blessing of our freedom and the freedom of future generations. This language was subsequently ordained and established the Constitution of these United States. The question is, what happened? The *Preamble* does not begin with "I wish" or "We prefer" or "We hope" or "My rights . . ." The *Preamble* is not precatory in nature. It establishes an agreement between and among the people of the United States of America. Additionally, the Preamble contains language which by its nature is transformational. The Preamble should inspire change or improvement in us all. The scope of its application is not restricted by time period or the nature of our circumstances. For anyone to engage in conduct that undermines or contradicts the *Preamble*, it is an affront and an injustice to Americans everywhere.

The meaning and purpose of the *Preamble* are undisputed and undeniable. The *Preamble's* mandate is clear. However, the decisions we make, and our subsequent conduct, often stray far from any attempt or desire to fulfill it. The United States has become a nation of citizens filled with, and sustained by, the contempt displayed toward the opinions and viewpoints of others, and untoward allegiances to extremism, which yields divisive and self-centered objectives. The only benefit to be gained by being so easily lured into such a lair is the satisfaction or justification it *may* provide us emotionally. Generally, if some action taken fills us with happiness, it must be good. If we experience disappointment, it must be bad. People are often motivated by, and find comfort in, their affective state of emotion, not in the pursuit of a principal or ideal which transcends our reliance on our emotions. As we become overwhelmed emotionally by fear, excitement, happiness, and the like, we tend to rely less on our innate abilities to reason, make decisions, and commit to a particular course of action. Allowing our insecurities to guide our decision-making does not honor the *Preamble*.

We are all insecure about something. People struggle over insecurities about their appearance, intelligence, station in life, etc. When these insecurities manifest, we are often exposed to bouts of uncertainty and self-doubt, which causes us to seek out satisfaction or comfort in a preferred state of emotion. Typically, we may become prone to acting impulsively to deal with the circumstances presented, rather than identifying and dealing with the source of it. Usually, a person in this position is not often equipped intellectually to identify and make changes about themselves or their circumstances. The tendency is to react to these unpleasant circumstances or conflict by casting blame, making excuses, expressing resentment, and hostility. Anyone who habitually conforms to exhibiting such reactive behavior will all too often fall short of adhering and honoring the vision and values of the *Preamble*. In all likelihood, it is beyond the capability of a person to understand and apply it to others, let alone themselves. The words of the *Preamble* should inspire us to want to be a better person each and every day. In order for each person to fulfill this shared mandate, it will require responding to a call that extends beyond a person's respective agenda or feelings. Simply, it cannot be done unless "We" are committed to live it out for the sake of our posterity. Otherwise, we will continue to fail in our responsibilities to prepare future generations to exercise their duty of citizenship.

Chapter III

Becoming Equipped

My brother and I were not the products of a wealthy family. Our parents did not live an extravagant lifestyle. I guess we would have been defined as a middle-class family. Our father, Girard Murphy was a highly skilled factory worker, Marine Corps veteran, a good provider, and a strong disciplinarian. He didn't make or accept excuses from my brother or me. In a nutshell, he could be terrifying. If you brought home a grade that was below his expectations, he was not pleasant to face after he arrived home from the plant. Our mother, Mary Helen Murphy was a dreamer, a visionary. She had aspirations for everyone. She was determined to make sure her husband and sons were properly positioned to be successful, whether it fit with any of our agendas or not. Throughout our childhood, our parents invested in us heavily. If my brother and I were a mutual fund or stock portfolio, our parents were determined to see a considerable return on their investment. In short, we were raised and prepared to confront and navigate the challenges associated with the seasons of our lives. We were not treated with kid gloves and told everything was going to be okay. They told us life would be tough on us. We were expected to successfully transition into adulthood and become men. We were incessantly reminded by our mother, "I am not taking care of grown folk!" If we failed, we were expected to suffer the consequences. If we fell, we were required to get back up. When we were teased or bullied, we were reminded that the world would be much tougher on us. To this day, I can hear my mother uttering the phrase, "Sticks and stones may break my bones, but names will never hurt me." I hated that phrase then, and I hate hearing it now. Nevertheless, she made her point.

If we met or exceeded our parents' expectations, we were not routinely rewarded with gifts or parties to celebrate every accomplishment. We didn't always receive a physical pat on the back. We were doing what we were expected to do. Parental acknowledgement and appreciation were often expressed with a smile and a tepid expression like "good job" or "congratulations." I don't recall hearing my parents use the proverbial phrase "I am proud of you" until I reached adulthood. When they said it then, and say it today, it has an importance that we cherish. Some might think this form of affirmation, or the lack thereof, is not sufficient to cultivate a child's confidence. It was for us. We had no choice. Our parents were able to effectively strike a unique balance between encouragement and restraint. It helped us to understand the importance of humility and how to exhibit confidence that does not require boasting or a display of arrogance. According to my mother, it was their job to make sure we didn't get a "big head." As we got older and accomplishments became more significant (e.g. college, law school, military graduations, etc.), their joy became more pronounced because they could see the fruit associated with their investment and our hard work.

Our parents understood that they could not afford to sugarcoat and hide the realities of this world from their sons. We were conditioned to understand how challenging life would be, and how our experiences would not be the same as our peers, especially our white counterparts. The 110% rule was in full effect in our household. Growing up, I routinely heard it from my mother. For a long period of time, I thought she made it up. I realized it was a principle of preparation and survival that was communicated to black children during the formative years. The 110% Rule was based on a belief that, to be considered on par or equally qualified as one's white peers, you had to exceed the norm and do extra. Simply, you had to be better.

For example, Mom and Dad were both sticklers for being on time. On time meant arriving early. Mom would always say be early for an appointment, never late. If you were required to be at work no later than 7:30 a.m., arrive no later than 7:00 a.m. If your white peers are earning B grades, you must earn an A. If your co-worker calls off from work repeatedly, you must show up every day without exception. The 110% Rule became deeply ingrained in me. I never forgot it. Unlike a lot of people today, I was taught to believe and understand that our destiny did not have to be determined by the ill-fated judgments and beliefs of others. Simply, don't make it easy for people to cast doubt on your intelligence and character.

This "Rule" has remained with me and helped guide and sustain me throughout my professional career. After I retired from the practice of law in 2017, the 110% Rule became less about competing with, or impressing, my white colleagues. Unbeknownst to me, this indoctrination by my parents provided me the impetus and motivation to develop and maintain a strong work ethic. Inevitably, it is that work ethic, not my race, that distinguishes me from my peers and colleagues.

The reality of the world for which my parents prepared us began to take shape for me in high school. I attended a parochial high school outside of Buffalo, New York. The demographic of the student body was predominantly white. Attending a predominantly white high school was challenging. Attending a catholic high school was different in so many respects. I did not understand anything about Catholicism. At that time in my life, I did not know any Catholics, especially black Catholics. I thought all black people attended black Baptist churches. As a part of the school's curriculum requirements, I was required to successfully complete theology classes each year. The classes focused on Catholicism, its traditions and rituals, and studying the Bible. This was the first time I was confronted with differences in church practices, preaching and teachings. I was unsure if I was supposed to go to mass, confession or accept communion. This was the first time I remember my parents, in particular my mother, encouraging me to look at it as though I was learning about another denomination. She said, "Just treat it like any other class." I didn't have to become Catholic to understand it. The most challenging part of this experience my first year was the questions I would be asked by my classmates. Many of them ranged from "How do you take communion? How are you baptized? Do people run around in your church?" Many of them had not known anyone black or attended a black church. All they could visibly relate my church experience to was a scene many of them watched from the movie *Blues Brothers* (1980), depicting a black church acting in an exaggerated worship. I had no idea what they were talking about. Questions like these became a regular occurrence, and when drawing distinctions between traditions, I would always be expected to answer questions and speak for the black church experience. None of my white peers were asked to speak about the process of confirmation and explain how to be a Eucharistic minister. I hated being placed in those circumstances. It was a very lonely and isolating experience. Mom would always say, "Elvage, they are asking because they are curious. They want to know." I did not want to be anyone's teacher. It didn't matter whether I liked it or not. It would become a regular occurrence. My brother and I both had to learn how not to be offended by questions from people outside our community who wish to understand our experiences.

Dad and Mom wanted me to get a good education. Attending a predominantly white school was not a guarantee that I would be successful. It did provide me a look into the minds and behavior of people I did not encounter every day. Dad said, "You need to learn how to interact with white folks confidently—that will command their respect. You gotta be prepared to deal with people outside your community and develop the skills to manage your discomfort. You do that by learning how to look people in their eyes when you speak to them."

I was among a few black students who commuted from the city of Buffalo to attend the school. I believed that I had a positive rapport with my classmates and most of my teachers. There was an atmosphere of racial tension within the school due to the closing and consolidation of other parochial high schools in the city of Buffalo and the subsequent reassignment of students of color to a high school unaccustomed to the significant presence of black males. Making the adjustment was easier for some of us than it was for others. I was making friends and settling in to the routine of school. Although I did not hate or fear white people, I was convinced they were not my friends. I did not see many of these students outside of school. I was merely going to school in their world. There were times when students would remind me that I was not welcome to become a part of it. Whenever I was observed speaking to another white female student, a white male student would tell me, "Elvage, that's my white meat. You messing with my white meat?" That was a clear message that I should keep my distance from and exercise caution when interacting with the white female students; and I did.

It was not until my junior year (1981-82) when white students began exhibiting an open hostility and indifference to me and my feelings. It was during my social studies class. I remember it was my favorite class. I sat in the front seat in the row next to the classroom window. I received good grades, and I liked my teacher. I raised my hand and was quick to volunteer and answer questions. A day I will remember vividly began with my teacher introducing the subject matter of slavery. I remember how he discussed it being immoral and illegal. He directed us to a page in our textbook, where he showed us an illustration in the textbook depicting the caricature of a slave being bound with shackles on his feet and hands. Then, it happened. A few students at the back of the room began laughing and making light of the illustration. The students began making statements like, "Slavery should be legal. I would have a slave if it were legal. Wouldn't you have a slave if it were legal Mr. _____?" He said, "No. It is immoral." Despite his efforts, the damage was done. The levity and freedom with which these students were making these statements, while laughing, hurt. It damaged me. I immediately lost my appetite for learning. Those few seconds tore at the core of my confidence. I lost interest in the class. I lost confidence in my teacher. I lost my enthusiasm for the subject matter. I hated it. Each and every day, I entered the class, sat down, placed my head on the desk, and turned it in the direction of the window at my left. My teacher never called on me again and never asked what was wrong. I can only surmise that he knew. Maybe he didn't know how to re-engage me. I don't recall saying another word in that class for the rest of the school year. My parents did notice my grade slipped in the class. My father asked, "Why did your grade go down in social studies? You had an A last quarter, now you have a B. Why?" I could not provide an acceptable response. He reminded me, "Elvage, you are a junior in high school. This is the year colleges look at to determine if they will admit you to their schools." Dad demanded I work harder. I did. But I never told my parents about what happened. Perhaps I should have told them. If I had, maybe I would have been spared the indignity of my father's wrath.

The indifference I experienced was not limited to the conduct of my fellow students. At the onset of my senior year (1982-83), I was looking forward to selecting and applying to colleges and universities. I had a meeting with one of the priests who served as the school's guidance counselor. While meeting with him, I advised him that I planned to attend college. After a brief discussion, he recommended that I consider attending a local community college or a vocational school. He felt this approach would be the best for me. Basically, he told me "Elvage, I do not think you are ready for a four-year school." He was not rude. He did not belittle me. At that moment, I was discouraged from applying to attend a four-year college or university. Following the meeting, I returned to class convinced that my guidance counselor's recommendation was correct. I had, for the moment, accepted his conclusion about my destiny. I remember telling some of my classmates who were told the same thing. We found solace and comfort knowing that we would be together the following year at a nearby community college. That plan came to a screeching halt that same evening, while I was having dinner with my parents and my brother, Terrance. The subject and content of my meeting with the guidance counselor was discussed. Then, I told my parents, "I am going to go to the local community college or a vocational school." All I can remember is my father's reaction. The sound of his voice was like the roar of a bear that shook the outer walls of our house. He said, "What are you talking about, boy! You have the brain to go to a four-year school. Why would you believe that mess? I don't care if he is the damn principal!" Dad was pissed. I have witnessed his anger before. But I don't recall ever seeing him that angry. Initially, I thought he was upset with the guidance counselor. I was wrong. He was more upset with me. At the time, I was scared. I had no idea what sent my father into this rage. Now, I understand. Dad may have been venting and directing his frustrations and anger toward me. In reality, his frustration and anger were being directed at a "white world" that was trying to pigeonhole his son and limit his opportunities. He knew I had expressed interest in becoming a lawyer. It was my idea not his. When I became older, I discovered my father aspired to be a lawyer. Had someone discouraged him from pursuing his dream? Were there obstacles placed in his path forbidding him from doing so? Did the circumstances of his life call him in another direction? Whatever the reason, there was no way he was going to allow me to fall prey to circumstances that would dissuade me from becoming a lawyer. That was the genesis of his anger and passion. I vividly remember his cheeks shaking and face turning a shade darker. I did not utter a word. I was in fear of what he might do next.

The lecture I received from my parents showed me how important it is to be mindful of the opinions and conclusions of the people who may be in a position to influence you. These individuals may be well-intentioned and believe they are acting in your best interest. "The road to hell is paved with good intentions." The opinions and advice of others must not determine our future. My father lovingly put his foot up my ass, redirected me, and made sure I did not depart from my goals or accept an outcome or an alternative that was not in line with them.

What would have happened if I did not have a father at this critical point in my development? What if my father, in particular, had not passionately reminded me of my potential and demanded that I not accept less than what I was capable of achieving? I believe the personal and professional consequences for me would have been devastating if my father had not jarred my senses to recognize and appreciate my potential to attend and graduate from a college and law school. I have to wonder how many black children (especially boys) are not receiving this type of intense, acute interaction from their father or an interested adult to diminish the impact of discouragement that is explicitly or implicitly communicated.

Mom's calm and supportive demeanor neutralized the tone of Dad's anger and frustration. She did not undermine or water down his message. I always wondered if Mom disagreed with how Dad handled the matter. If she did, she never let it show. She did not protect me from his anger. She did not contradict him. She did not attempt to offer my father an explanation on my behalf. As a moment of silence presented, my mother, in a very calm and determined tone, affirmed my father's position. To the best of my recollection, she told me, "Your father just wants you understand you cannot accept what these white folks tell you. Your guidance counselor doesn't know you. He doesn't know your family. People don't know what you are capable of achieving. You can't allow anyone to define you or determine your destiny." I also remember Mom saying, "There are people in this world who think they know what is best for you. They may mean well. Some will not. But it doesn't make them right or mean they know what is best for you!"

This was a reminder that well-intentioned people do not necessarily operate in your best interest. They can dissuade or discourage us from pursuing our goals and dreams. My parents saw the need to make sure we didn't submit to the definitions and opinions of others. Our lives and our futures depended upon it. I can only imagine how many other people in towns like Erie have been discouraged and redirected from their life's purpose by the advice of some well-intentioned, albeit short-sighted, individuals.

During the early stages of my career as a prosecutor, I would arrive at work around 7:30 a.m. Most days, I would return home by no later than 6:00 p.m. My wife would have dinner prepared, and we would have dinner with our son, who was eight years old at the time and our daughter, who was four years of age. Following dinner, my wife would go to work, and I would remain home to clean the kitchen and help our son and daughter with homework my wife could not help them complete—get them prepared and put them down for bed, and then work on case files until my wife returned home. The pursuit of the "American Dream" in our house was just trying to make it through the day and make sure our son and daughter had enough food and clothing. At the time, the best we could aspire for was to pay our rent and other bills on time. Being confined to our existing job duties was not something my wife and I aspired to do. We were ambitious. We remained diligent and committed to fulfilling our job responsibilities. I also performed a lot of community service and coached my kids' soccer and basketball teams. Nevertheless, we remained committed to being the predominant source of our children's moral development. We helped our children understand the societal differences they would encounter by answering questions about why a neighbor child's father did not live with them, or why they were told by other children, "I can't play with you because you're black." Our children were fortunate. Their mother and father were married and present every day in the same household to help them both navigate the issues life would bring before them. In addition, our son and daughter maintained relationships with their maternal and paternal grandparents, great-grandmothers, and a great-great grandmother, as well as their aunts, uncles, and cousins. Although our son and daughter witnessed the differences in their parents' personalities and opinions, they saw their parents struggle and work as a unit to achieve a single-minded purpose: to raise and equip them. Our marriage was not without its challenges. There was never a doubt that my wife and I were committed to one another and to our children's upbringing. Their interests were our highest priority. Like my parents, my wife and I, who are as different as different can be, functioned to successfully prepare our children to transition into adulthood.

As I think back on this time, James and Heléna were, and remain, our "American dream." I don't recall using words from the *Preamble* with my then four-year-old daughter and eight-year-old son. But those words and their meaning were clearly reflected in the relationships we had with them. They both looked to us for guidance and, most importantly, fun. To not fulfill our parental responsibilities would have been the greatest breach of the core values of the *Preamble*. Fulfilling this call required compromise and making sacrifices. Selfishness does not fall by the wayside when you are a twenty-seven-year-old father of two children. Career advancement, wealth, and notoriety were priorities. I believed it was my role to provide for my family. It was difficult, though. Our son and daughter had different interests and expectations. Nothing mattered more to them than to have their mother and father at home. Although promotions and financial remuneration followed, I had to learn to gear down my ambitions and operate within a narrower realm that would not compromise our marriage and the upbringing of our children.

I am grateful to my father. He set the standard for hard work, *sacrifice*, and honor. He never wavered in the fulfillment of his duty as a father. He worked every day, returned home every afternoon, attended our baseball games, monitored our schoolwork, and did it again the next day. He made sacrifices. Dad is brilliant on so many levels. My mother would say, "Your father could be a millionaire." She was right. Dad should have been a lawyer or a United States Congressman or Senator. He was a skilled tradesman, who could have opened his own business. Yet, none of it mattered more than raising his boys. He was my example of a father. He was not a perfect person. Yet, he was a perfect father because he was home and actively present in our lives. His personal sacrifices for us have been immense. He remains supportive and has encouraged us to be this way for our own children.

Children have needs. Adults have wants. Admittedly, it took me a little longer to come to the realization that my ambitions must not take precedence over my children's needs. My wife helped me to weigh the cost and benefits of what was truly important. It was an analysis we engaged in together. In the long term, I knew it is more important to leave money and other opportunities on the table, in order to be at home. Our son and daughter routinely acknowledge the magnitude of the sacrifices we made on their behalf. They honor us with their lives. Most importantly, they appreciate and love the person they see in the mirror.

Chapter IV
Something's not right

I recite the Pledge of Allegiance with my students every morning. I was raised to believe and trust in God. I am a Christian. But when I was thirteen years old, I began to have questions in the belief or mantra that America is "one nation under God, indivisible, with liberty and justice for all," and that America has always been a Christian nation from its inception. I have no doubt that, when it was formed, the people traditionally identified as America's founding fathers and mothers believed it, and attempted to live accordingly. However, it is not a secret that our country has not lived up to the Christian principles I hear white conservative Christians championing. My mother made sure my brother and I went to church. I believe the Bible is the only source of God's Word and that His Word and prayer are the mediums by which we get to know him and maintain our relationship with Him. Yet, when interacting with white Christians, who purportedly read the same Bible, believe in the same God, and that Jesus Christ, His Son, gave his life for the remission of our sins, there has always been a disconnect between me and my white Christian brothers and sisters. For years, I thought it was all on me. To some degree, it was. I was the product of different experiences and perspectives. Throughout the early phase of my faith walk, the issues that took center stage in our church were social justice, fighting racism and overcoming discrimination, securing a good education, and economic empowerment. Many of these issues were the genesis of the sermons that were preached and reflected my experiences. When I was growing up, I do not recall issues like abortion, homosexuality, and preserving prayer in public schools, albeit important, being the primary issues of concern at my church and in my household growing up. I don't recall these issues having a direct impact on my family or the black community. Thus, I surmised that the concerns and priorities of black and white Christians were different. To me, this was an irreconcilable paradox. For example, I don't recall black ministers or black Christians from my childhood discussing the moral implications and the damage associated with abortions and the absence of prayer from public schools. I don't recall white Christians standing and calling for the end the disenfranchisement of poor black people in America or speaking out against police brutality. As a thirteen-year-old boy in 1978, I could not understand or appreciate the differences between white and black Christians. To me, we should have been on the same side: God's side. Yet, we were not. From my perspective, if truth is truth, these issues should have been of concern to every Christian who purported to live by these sacred Christian values.

As my questions increased, my father sought to help me understand this inconsistency by telling me there was more hypocrisy in the church than in any other institution in America. Dad always remained consistent about his beliefs, and his behavior conformed to them. When he encountered people who claimed to have certain moral standards and beliefs to which their behavior did not conform, they were "hypocrites." Our father could tolerate a lot of people and situations. Hypocrisy and hypocrites did not make the cut. I do believe that is why Dad was resistant to attending church when we were younger. He saw hypocrisy in those who occupied the pulpit, and he hated it. His lesson transformed into a tirade and rants about how church people are the biggest hypocrites. According to Dad, "Church people attempt to hold people to a standard they cannot, or will not, live up to themselves." From that moment, I knew what ailed the church and a lot of people from doing the right thing: it was hypocrisy. Mom would interject defensively and offer the opinion that there is hypocrisy everywhere. "Girard, not all church people are hypocrites." This was to be expected. Her father served as a minister-evangelist. Dad would quickly respond and reaffirm his original position that there is more hypocrisy in the church. "Well, maybe not, but most of them are hypocrites!" Simply, it was a typical energetic Murphy family discussion.

Dad's hatred of hypocrisy is understandable. He considered it the equivalent of a lie. To him, lying is a form of selfishness that inevitably causes harm. Dad expected people he encountered to be truthful and consistent at all times. He measures everyone by this standard. There are no exceptions. My father could tell a lot about someone who did not keep their word or look him in the eyes. If you said you were going to be at a particular location at a particular time, you better be there. If you told him you were going to do something, do it. If I ever gave my father an "excuse" why I did not do something, Dad would say, "Boy! Don't give me that crap!" or "Don't tell me what you are going to do, just do it!" The only thing that rivaled my father's intimidating presence was his belief in honor. He measured himself and others by it. He expected his sons to live by the same code.

Dad believes it is important to make sacrifices to help others and do the right thing. He does not tolerate people who take advantage of others or those he describes as phonies. Dad and Mom can spot a phony instantly. It's a trait my brother and I have inherited. Dad also has an intense passion for justice. Treating other people fairly matters to him. Although he never complained about the things that happened to him, the injustices displayed toward others have tested his faith in our nation's institutions, and those who have sworn an oath to protect and defend others.

Dad doesn't believe in accepting the status quo. If change is needed, he believes in taking a stance and supporting others who are willing to make the personal and professional sacrifices needed to see change come to pass. He doesn't just sit, rant, and rave. He takes action. He never hesitated to donate his money and talent for a cause that represented his passions. He is a man of action, who continues to invest in his family's hopes and dreams. He does not believe or invest in lost causes. His investments have yielded efforts and initiatives that are in line with his expectations to help make the lives of others better than his own. Dad's actions continue to reflect his values and beliefs.

Dad believes in education. He invested in our education and in the education of his grandchildren. Dad believes in being responsible. His devotion and loyalty know no bounds. Even after my parents divorced, Dad continued to look out for our mother's interest and provide her help financially if she needed it. As I attempted to bring a golf program with a national affiliation to children in the city of Erie, it was Dad who made the initial financial investment in the initiative to help a local nonprofit organization to introduce elementary- and middle-school-aged children to the game of golf. When I became a judicial candidate, it was my father who traveled to be at my campaign kick-off. He attended fundraisers, and provided me with much-needed support. After remarrying, my father's second wife, Mother Rae, was diagnosed with a terminally ill disease during the second year of their marriage. Throughout her hospitalization and home care, Dad remained at her side. He helped bathe her, get her in and out of bed, made her meals, and transported her to and from her chemotherapy appointments. He never wavered in his devotion, and after Mother Rae was placed in hospice, he remained at her side until she passed away.

Hypocrisy does not equate with Dad's sense of devotion and loyalty. Admittedly, it took me a while to appreciate the trust people place in the consistency of another person's conduct and how critical it is to defining a person's character and reputation. Dad's expectations set a standard I dare not disregard. I learned the importance of honoring every commitment and making sure my actions did my speaking for me.

In 2002, I received an offer to teach at a local university. As I approached the start of a new career in higher education, I viewed it as an opportunity to have a positive impact on young people and produce, in others, the qualities and attributes I believed would propel them to a successful career. Much to my surprise, the academic environment did not reflect the level of professionalism and collegiality I expected. I was naïve to the degree of hypocrisy that was being exhibited among colleagues and administrators. The hypocrisy, like racism, is not always readily apparent. It is covert and is only exposed when it causes irreparable damage or undermines the aspirations of impressionable people who place their minds and hearts in the hands of those who are entrusted to teach them.

I entered academia from the day-to-day grind of practicing law. At the time I was approached by representatives of my former university about accepting a tenure track position, I was in the process of transitioning out of my role as an Assistant Public Defender to begin a private practice. Although I had taught at other colleges and universities as an adjunct, becoming a college professor was never on my radar. Initially, I did wonder that, if I became an educator, would I become one of those people who teach because they can't do instead of being one of those who can? Becoming an educator was so far off my radar. After discussing it with Janel, we both realized it would present a great opportunity for our family. In addition, I thought working in education would be a welcome change from the adversarial posturing of working in a courtroom every day. Never had I been so wrong. Following the interview process, I was offered a tenure track appointment and subsequently accepted it. As I transitioned into my new position, I encountered a minority of colleagues who were adamantly opposed to my hiring and openly expressed doubts about my expertise and ability to successfully transition into academia. They made every effort to undermine my standing with students, as well as my future applications for tenure and promotion. As this disdain from select colleagues grew, twelve years later, a more collegial member of our department's faculty informed me that one of my disgruntled colleagues had referred to me as the department's "affirmative action hire." The attitudes and conduct of some of my colleagues elucidated a nature contrary to their public personas within the university community. Thanks to Dad and Mom, I had been prepared to handle such circumstances and navigate the attitudes exhibited by a few white colleagues who thought it was their job to keep me where they believed I belonged.

My chief concern was always for the students. My performance evaluations and student evaluations ranged from very good to excellent to superior. My mother and father always told me, "Elvage, you have to keep your eye on the prize." Mom, in particular, would say, "Kill your enemies with kindness and do not give them anything, no matter how minor, to use against you." Every detail became important. Every action I took was measured. I arrived early. I stayed late and performed well above the minimum expectations of my peers. In addition, I enjoyed my work, performed my tasks, and assumed responsibility for projects that others felt were beneath them and refused to accept. The most important step I took was becoming student-centered. I can say with certainty that every moment of engagement with students allowed me to demonstrate a commitment and passion for their best interest, development and success. My actions were consistent with my beliefs. When I told my students I would do something on their behalf or at their request, they could count on me to be true to my word. Nevertheless, this didn't stop a few of my wayward colleagues from engaging in cryptic discussions with students about the subject matter I was teaching, and if I was regularly showing up for my classes.

I was not surprised by the actions of some of "my colleagues." They were self-described liberal or progressive white males who claimed to champion the importance of diversity and inclusion by mentoring the junior "colored" faculty. Admittedly, I could have benefitted from the guidance. However, I felt the degree of submission they required from me was too high a price to pay. These men were motivated by what Mom would say, "Elvage, it's jealousy"—a typical Mom response that had a basis of truth. The ugliness and resentment of these men were spurred by their own professional inadequacies and shortcomings. In an attempt to not allow frustration with this group of "learned men" to permeate and continue to poison our department, I attempted to reach out and discuss this matter with the ringleader. I knew it was not in the best interest of our department to allow this discontent to continue. I didn't want to be viewed as a contributor to the divisiveness I had no role in creating. Dad and Mom would always say, "It's not fair. Oftentimes, we (black people) carry the burden of making peace." I hated hearing and being reminded of it. I always felt like it placed me in a subservient or weaker position to my white peers. Regardless of how offended I was by the thought of reaching out, I approached this particular colleague and expressed my concerns to him about the need to reconcile our differences, and that it is in the best interest of our students. I said, "Every member of our department has something of value to offer to our students and program. We all have unique areas of expertise, and my contribution should not be dismissed because I do not have the traditional terminal degree." He informed me, "Elvage, you are being sensitive." No matter how many times I confronted a white person about some aspect of their behavior, this was the typical response I would receive. I became accustomed to hearing this response from white people whenever I had enough respect for them to address an issue of concern. I just looked at him and walked backed to my office, shaking my head in disbelief. A student was waiting in front of my office door and required my assistance. It was the best thing that could have happened. For a moment, I forgot about me and the frustration I was experiencing. I managed my anger and shifted my attention to a student with whom my conduct would have the greatest impact. I had to exhibit dignity and grace when I came face to face with this student. I realized it was a victory for which I would not receive public acknowledgment or applause. The student had no idea what I had just experienced. It was a moment I could have given in to something less dignified and allowed it to negatively impact an opportunity to positively engage and assist a student in need. This was the beginning of a very important lesson for me personally and professionally.

Due to my legal and trial experience, I was trained to argue and win. In this case, I realized I didn't have to win an argument with someone who was not receptive to having a discussion. Winning or being told I was right by this colleague was not as important to me as I originally believed. I knew I was not being treated fairly by him and others. At that moment, it was more important for me to live up to the commitment I made to my students and to bring honor to my parents who prepared me to navigate this type of nonsense. Rising above the fray was a lesson I learned during my days as a prosecutor. Now, it was more important than succumbing to it. To do otherwise would have been selfish and hypocritical. I know the manner in which I handled that interaction with my colleague brought honor to my family, and all of my colleagues, even the ones whose hearts were filled with jealously and resentment.

In 2012, I was elected to be the Chairperson of my academic department. At the time of my election, I had been employed at the university for ten years. Between 2002-12, I was awarded tenure, and promoted to the rank of Associate and Full Professor, respectively. One year into my term, I attended a meeting with other department chairs and the university's Provost. Our university was experiencing a decline in enrollment and a budget shortfall. Faculty layoffs were under consideration. Any and every theory that could be offered to explain the decline in enrollment was considered and debated. According to some evidentiary-based data, the decline in enrollment was being attributed to a corresponding decline in the region's high school graduation rates, antiquated degree programs, exorbitant faculty salaries, etc. There was one area in my opinion that made the aforementioned evidentiary-based data pale in comparison. It was an area no one (faculty and administrators) wanted to acknowledge or discuss. It was a question I believed warranted serious consideration. Had our commitment to student engagement waned? Had we departed from our mission, abandoned our values, and compromised our vision? These were questions I asked myself based on my daily interaction with students. There wasn't a concern that students weren't willing to share with me. At the time, I wasn't sure if this was a good thing or not. It was exhausting. Oftentimes, there were complaints regarding a disagreement with their instructor over an exam grade or the lack of assistance received from a financial aid officer. Although the nature of the complaints may have been inconsequential to me personally, there were concerns that students felt we would routinely display attitudes of indifference. As Department Chair, you see and become aware of issues among the faculty and the students under your charge that you'd wish you hadn't. It makes you ask, "What the hell was my colleague thinking? Why would he or she treat or speak to a student in that manner?" Even after approaching and attempting to discuss matters informally with colleagues, I was surprised by how unwilling some were to accept responsibility and make common sense changes to conform to our university's mission. One of my former colleagues would repeatedly remind us, "We have the best jobs on the planet." He was correct then, and now. Much of what concerned me was the realization that students were being treated as a means to an end, and their value marginalized.

Anytime I or other colleagues of the university community raised concerns about faculty not adhering to their academic advising and teaching duties, the concerns did not always get the attention they warranted. Were they being summarily ignored or dismissed? Who knows? It became evident that some members of our faculty, staff, and administration were not comfortable addressing these issues, although protocols were in place to do so. I asked myself, "Did we lose sight of the institution's mission, vision and values? In all fairness, six different presidents in seventeen years did not help with our university's continuity and stability. It made it challenging to hold personnel accountable. We should have been called into account. We were not. The only time the institution's values and mission became important (at least to some members of the faculty) was when the collective bargaining agreement would be on the verge of expiring. Like clockwork, select faculty members, who would not ordinarily make time to assist students, would be the first to stress how important it is to get students on our side to provide us with the leverage we needed to avert a work stoppage and force our state system back to the negotiating table. Ironically, it would be the same faculty members who had a reputation for the mistreatment of students who would consider it imperative to garner student support for a new contract. How can any institution expect to experience financial stability and prosperity while operating under such a cloud of hypocrisy it's unwilling to remove? It cannot.

For seventeen years, I have witnessed and experienced the best higher education has to offer. And if there is one conclusion I have reached, no family, educational institution, government, and nation can sustain itself and experience growth and prosperity if the values and mission for its existence are not honored by the people entrusted with fulfilling them. The manner in which we conduct ourselves in public is a reflection of how we conduct our private lives. Our public and private lives are inextricably linked. No matter how much we try, our true character is inevitably revealed. Where there is a lack of continuity and consistency between our public and private lives, impressionable people are likely to become confused and discouraged. Who and what to trust are permanently and detrimentally impacted. Many of my former university colleagues lived their lives in a vacuum. They were incapable or unwilling to give proper consideration to their thoughts and actions and its consequences without setting aside their need and preference to maintain the status quo. It was an epiphany I would soon experience with one of my own students.

A black female student helped me understand that I was not doing a good job of being consistent with my public representations. I vividly recall teaching a section of *Introduction to Criminal Justice*. I was teaching on the United States federal and state court systems. A young woman raised her hand and asked a question for clarification. According to her, I exhaled a noticeable "sigh." Before I could answer her question, she asked, "Why are you getting frustrated?" Remarkably, I did not notice it until she brought it to my attention. Although I was able to dissuade her concern and answer her questions, that moment caused me to re-evaluate the nature of my responses to inquiries, and to become conscientious of the way I would respond to questions in the future. I realized I had an impatient temperament. I vividly remember seeing the frustration and anxiety emitted on this student's face. These were expressions I did not want to become a regular occurrence. I knew steps needed to be taken to regulate my mannerisms and body language to prevent me from exhibiting a scintilla of frustration toward my students ever again.

Educators must become self-aware of their personal and professional development. When I began my university teaching career, I fell into the habit of being critical of students for coming into my office and asking me for information about the operation of the university, curriculum requirements, internships, etc. when this information was readily available on a bulletin board outside my door or could be perused by accessing the university's webpage. Then, I remembered it is my responsibility to be there for students. They do not exist to make my life easier, no matter how minor I may perceive their need for assistance. I "quickly" realized what I was missing. If a person is looking for guidance and direction, that moment of interaction, no matter how short, has the potential to leave him or her a favorable and important impression that may be an example of something they can remember and exemplify later in life. We often take for granted the opportunities we have to make an impression on another individual. When we decide to be rude, ridicule or criticize someone, brush his or her concerns aside to move on to something else, we do it for the sake of our convenience. Once I learned this lesson, education became and remains a significant part of my life's mission and purpose. No student should be viewed as a subject of irritation, or a means to an end. Young people seek guidance and direction. They will respond to timely encouragement, and advice if we are prepared to fulfill our role as educators.

My conservative colleagues blame the large composition of liberal faculty, and the "growing moral confusion . . . [being taught] among college students,"[1] as a problem in higher education. I am not convinced the large composition of liberal faculty and what they're teaching ade-

---

1. Feazel and Swain, pg. 218

quately addresses all the problems in higher education. Much of what transpires in these classrooms and faculty offices are a product of the unwillingness of administrators to exhibit the courage to take action against employees who are not willing to fulfill their duties or mission as educators. There are some administrators in higher education who are adept and comfortable shifting personnel responsibilities to their various academic departments, rather than exhibiting and maintaining an exemplary standard of accountability to address issues under the scope of their authority. Additionally, when some administrators attempt to wield their influence, they do so strategically to leverage outcomes that serve their personal and professional interests, and often it can be at the expense of the best interests of students and faculty who are truly committed to the noble calling of education.

No institution or company can prosper when difficult circumstances arise, and there is no infrastructure in place to guarantee that truth and justice are valued. I am reminded of the Bible verse, "For they sow the wind, and they shall reap the whirlwind."[2] Declining enrollment and an uncertain future is what many institutions of higher learning have reaped due to the nature of the seeds sown. America is in a similar state. Our growth and prosperity are being hindered due to the widespread hypocrisy that permeates our most sacred institutions. I can see why Dad abhors hypocrisy. It is dangerous, destructive and dishonors the provisions of the *Preamble*.

---

2. NIV Bible, Book of Hosea Chapter 8: Verse 7

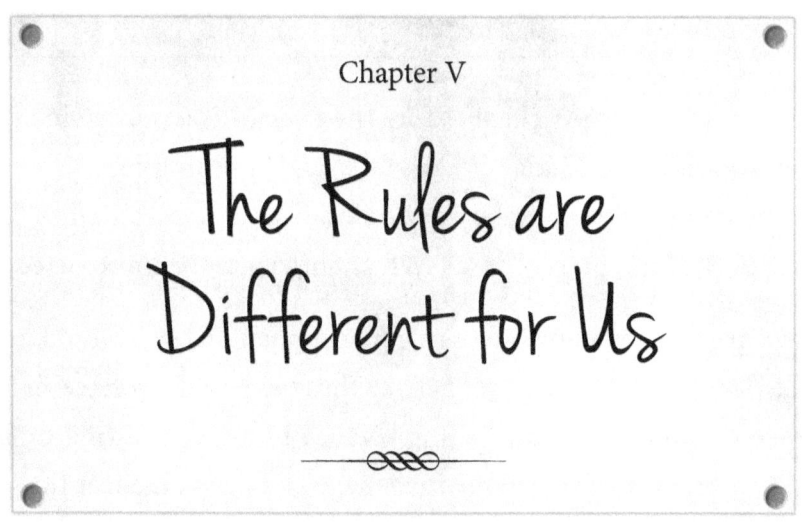

Chapter V
The Rules are Different for Us

I cannot cite the exact moment and time that Mom and Dad supplemented their teaching to the 110% Rule. They told me, "In this world, there are rules for white people and rules for black people, and you have to be prepared when the rules of the game change." I always knew and operated with the mindset that fairness is not guaranteed. If it happens, good. If it does not, don't be surprised. Dad said, "Boy, you must be prepared for the unexpected and adapt to the circumstances." I didn't like uncertainty or the waiting that went along with it. Learning how to be prepared offset the element and impact of surprises as a trial lawyer, or when I was asked to deliver impromptu remarks to an audience.

Throughout my legal career, I have represented clients from all walks of life. I received phone calls or requests from people for legal representation in parts of rural Pennsylvania that no other black attorney would dare take. I was initially reluctant to take many of these cases. But I was motivated to provide assistance, and I believed that my representation would help, but also impact and shape, the lives of people who rarely interacted with black people. As I engaged the representation of each client before the court, I was surprised at the graciousness of most judges, their staffs, and opposing counsel. These experiences taught me to be open-minded and be prepared to seize the opportunities presented, as well as anticipate the unexpected.

I have grown accustomed to being put in positions that would make most people cringe and avoid. And these experiences have helped shaped me to understand the importance of not submitting to fear. Dad and Mom encouraged me to manage and overcome fear through the acquisition of knowledge, taking calculated risks, and presenting myself thoughtfully and intelligently. The following examples illustrate how these lessons proved valuable.

In the spring of 2011, I was representing a young man convicted of the aggravated assault of his infant son. At the time of his sentencing hearing, the sentencing judge came on to the bench. After addressing a few housekeeping measures in open court, the judge pontificated in open court about the severity of the injuries sustained by the infant child. He turns to me and asks, "Attorney Murphy, on a scale of one to ten, how would you rate the seriousness of the injuries sustained by this child?" At that moment, it appeared like time had slowed, and all eyes were on me. I became very angry with the judge. Words came to mind that I dared not utter. I could not believe he was asking me a question that placed me in the unenviable position of providing a statement he could effectively use to my client's detriment, justifying the imposition of a harsher sentence. No matter the number I would select from his scale, I knew the result would be catastrophic to my client's appeal. Then, I heard the words of my father, "Elvage, do not let them see you sweat. Stay calm, think and the words will come to you." I recall taking a deep breath. I made eye contact with a clerk from the Erie County Clerk's office. I raised my head and said, "Judge, asking me to assign a numeric value to the injuries sustained by my client's son would trivialize the nature of this child's injuries." The judge looked at me. He turned and looked at the prosecutor. The judge made no further reference to the matter and, shortly thereafter, imposed the sentence.

What I experienced before this particular judge on that morning was something I will never forget. I thought to myself, how on Earth could a judge expect a criminal defense attorney, who has an ethical obligation to his client, be expected to honor it by answering such a question? Providing even a tacit response to the judge's question could have very easily subjected me, as well as co-counsel, to claims of ineffective assistance of counsel. In this situation, the justice associated with the sentencing proceeding took a back seat to a judge's need for self-aggrandizement. Although the imposition of the sentence against my client was well within the range of what the law allowed, the behavior exhibited by the judge during that proceeding was devoid of the expectations legal practitioners would otherwise expect of someone serving as a judge. The judge intended to play to the emotions of those who were understandably concerned for the welfare of a child. This type of judicial behavior is dangerous and routinely exhibited by judges who seek a level of notoriety from the general public they cannot seem to live without. They forget that, while serving in a prominent position, it is one that should be performed in relative obscurity.

In 2015, I was one of eight candidates for two county judicial positions. The local bar association sponsored a luncheon and provided each candidate a brief time period to introduce their candidacy, their background, qualifications, and the reasons why they were running for the positions. All candidates were informed that the speeches would be videotaped and made available by the 2015 Judicial Plebiscite Committee for the benefit of the voters of Erie County. Before the luncheon, candidates were notified that lots would be drawn and each candidate would be notified prior to their arrival in which order they would be called to speak. Prior to my arrival, I had not received any notification by phone or email. I sat down at my seat. I recall a plate of food being placed before me. Soon thereafter, the presentations began. Since I had not been notified of when my name would be called, I prepared to be called first. I was not called. As the first candidate spoke, I prepared to be second. I was not called. As the second candidate spoke, I prepared to be third. I was not called. This pattern continued. I remember seething on the inside, while maintaining a smile. People in that room knew I was a very good public speaker because they have seen me present in court and speak at other venues. I was determined to let it rip when my time came. Finally, I was announced: "Last, but not least, Attorney Elvage Murphy." Although I was still fuming, I stepped to the microphone and said, "Well, Momma always said, 'You save the best for last.'" I looked out on the audience, and they looked more nervous than I did. I began my speech by telling the audience, "I am running for the position of Erie County Court of Common Pleas because I believe in the search for truth and justice." From that point on, I saw people in the audience responding nervously, shifting in their seats, and whispering to their colleagues. It didn't matter. I was determined to represent what I stood for and hoped to scare the hell out of them. I was convinced my speech would resonate with the general public when it was released. People who didn't know me would see how easily I distinguished myself from the other candidates. Following the luncheon, I anticipated the video presentations would be released. Days following the luncheon, candidates were later notified there was a change in plans and the video presentations of each candidate would not be made available. I'm not sure what happened. But it didn't surprise me in the least. I was prepared for the rules to change. Maybe it was a technical glitch. I don't know. All I know is I did not fail to perform and present my candidacy when my time came. I did not complain. I did not ask why I was not extended the courtesy of being notified where I was slotted to present. The people who coordinated the event knew what happened, and why.

If there is anything I learned from my experience being a candidate for public office, it's that politics can bring you in contact with some caring and aspirational people. However, the world of politics is fluid. When people believe what belongs to them is threatened, they will take steps, albeit innocent ones, to neutralize and place others at a disadvantage. What members of my former legal community didn't recognize is that I was born and raised by a family and in a community where I was inspired to believe I could overcome obstacles and represent the best of who I am and who my parents raised me to become.

At the time I was in the midst of engaging this project, I was in Buffalo, New York, visiting my father. While awaiting his arrival, I decided to go to a local grocery store. I didn't know this short ride would provide me an opportunity to encounter and have a brief reunion with one of my childhood friends, Paul. Paul and I lived nearby in the same North Buffalo neighborhood. For the next twenty to thirty minutes, the substance of our conversation was part jovial (primarily due to the surprise reunion); it was also empowering and enlightening (primarily to him). As we began to discuss the roads we took in life, we also began discussing the current social and racial climate in America. He was surprised that I had become an attorney. Even more surprising was his reaction when I shared the racial hostility I faced practicing law in Erie. The conversation shifted to our old neighborhood and the kids with whom we were mutually acquainted.

We, along with other groups of kids in the neighborhood, played basketball, football, baseball, etc. As we all grew older, some of these impromptu pickup games would invoke disagreements, resentment, and statements that would divide us among racial lines. His response was, "It is interesting to hear you say that because I didn't think things like that happened to you." I said, "Really, why would you think I never experienced those sort of issues?" He said, "I just didn't think you did. I never saw you get angry." I went on the explain to him, "Paul, our parents always said the best way to respond to bigotry and racism is to never give ignorant people the pleasure of getting under your skin or making you upset. They expected us to deal with the ignorance of others directly without compromising our intelligence and dignity. From their perspective, there was never an acceptable reason to succumb to ignorance."

There were a lot of times when my brother and I didn't comply with our parents' expectations. We were young, emotional, often easily offended, loud, and opinionated; loud and opinionated are traits of Murphy men. When either of us were called n____r, it made us less amenable to these lessons. Mom and Dad helped us to understand that strength requires discipline, and discipline is strength under control. It takes discipline to understand the world we live in. Mom said, "I am not raising you to be a n____r in the street." Whenever we fell short of their expectations, our parents were quick to express their disappointment and held us accountable for our behavior. They weren't concerned about our reasons or the excuses we offered to justify our reactions. Once, I remember getting into a fight, and I told my father, "I had to defend my pride." For some reason, I thought that explanation would fly with him. I had never been so wrong. He said, "Boy! What pride? You haven't done anything to make or defend a claim of pride!" After he sarcastically belittled my explanation, he made sure I realized I had no pride to defend.

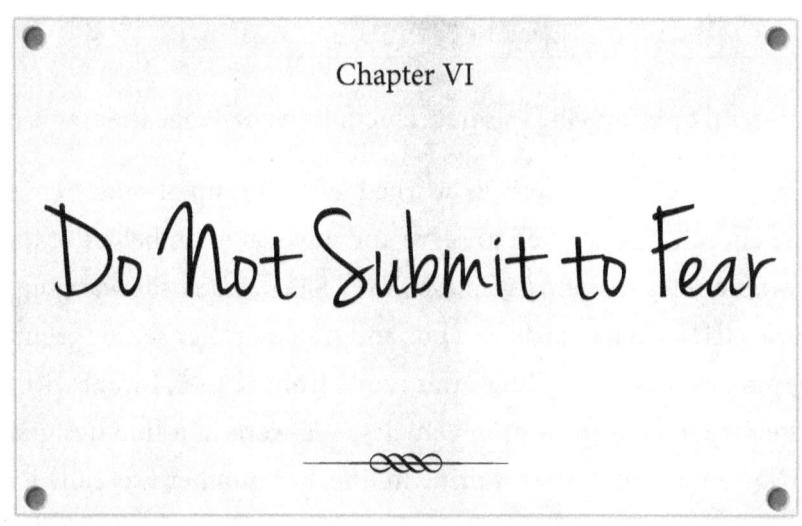

Chapter VI
Do Not Submit to Fear

Fear is a powerful inducement. Fear can create indifference, polarize, and destroy communities. Fear may also foster our acquisition of knowledge and wisdom, as well as compel us to take actions necessary to fulfill our legal or moral obligations. It can also provide insightful individuals the impetus they need to move forward and embrace change. The question is to which are you most likely to submit?

When we were younger, my brother and I believed our mother was fearless. I saw her stand up to black men who disrespected her and white men who tried to demean her. We would say, "Ma is crazy" or "Ma is trippin" to describe her behavior at times. I often thought her fearlessness bordered on being reckless. Her "fearlessness" would often embarrass us and inspire us at the same time. In retrospect, I would describe this fearlessness or recklessness differently. Mom was bold! There wasn't any question she would not ask, or assertion she would not make, if she believed it would better position herself and her family. She established quite a reputation for herself within our family and church. On more than one occasion, I have heard people say, "Ms. Murphy don't play." I have no doubt this was, and remains, a universal opinion. She was not reluctant to challenge the status quo.

I remember when she actively worked with a group of senior citizens at the church. She worked to serve and advocated on behalf of them. She would refer to them as "my seniors." She decided she was going to secure a CDL license to drive a bus and transport her senior group on shopping excursions. While I was home from school, I went with her to the Department of Motor Vehicles. We were in a line designated for CDL applicants. After waiting in line, her number was called, and she approached one of the employees. My mother inquired into the process of acquiring her CDL license. The white male employee was less than enthusiastic to provide her the information he had willingly and *voluntarily* provided the male customer who preceded her. Mom could have taken it as a personal affront and cussed out the employee. She could have accused him of being a racist. I watched as she remained calm and asked thoughtful questions to receive the guidance and direction to which she and any other applicant would ordinarily be entitled. At the conclusion of the interaction, she turned around, looked at me, and said, "A woman has to ask questions just to get the same information a man willingly volunteers to another man." Had this worker assumed my mother would not be a viable candidate for a commercial driver's license because she was a woman and black? It's possible. Was this worker's experience with CDL applicants limited to primarily male candidates? It's possible. What lesson did I learn? You cannot be expected to receive the same treatment and privileges graciously extended to others. Fairness is often a concept applied relative to the experiences of the person who is entrusted with employing it. You must make your interests and desires known and pursue your ambitions with vigor. This was the first time I witnessed my mother experiencing this form of treatment. I saw in my mother a determination to acquire knowledge to which she knew she was entitled, in order for her to become equipped and empowered to serve others. Mom refused to submit to fear.

Mom also demonstrated a propensity to interject herself in situations on the street, even if it placed her in harm's way. She would not allow an injustice or the mistreatment of another person to go unaddressed. If something was taking place in her presence that offended her sensibilities, she confronted it.

When I was ten years old, my brother and I were walking with my father and mother to a nearby restaurant to get ice cream. Mom saw boys doing something they had no business doing. She would move in to do some "street mothering." She did not know the boys or their parents. Nothing could stop her from intervening. If she observed anyone's child engaging in foolishness, it set her off and motivated her to take action. Fortunately, my father stepped in and stopped her. Dad said, "Mary, you can't go and get involved in that mess. You don't know how those boys are going to react." Generally, Mom's reactive nature to get involved trumped the type of fear that would ordinarily create indifference or inaction. Mom's genuine passion for the welfare of others never waned.

There wasn't any place she would not go. From the time we could walk, my mother believed in our family having experiences that would prepare us for life as adults. She believed in the "fine dining" experiences. During the 1970s, we would get dressed up and go to local, upscale restaurants. At the time, I didn't appreciate the significance of this dining-out experience. I don't remember seeing a lot of other black kids doing this kind of thing with their parents. Today, I realize that some black families may not have had these types of formal dining experiences for fear of how they might be received. To this day, I still have to remain committed to overcome the fear of entering an establishment not typically frequented by black people due to its location or the predominant race of its patrons. Mom was preparing us to be comfortable in our skin wherever we went.

Mom's strength is her confidence. She exhibited a level of confidence that allowed her to navigate any room, no matter the make up of the people within it. She didn't have to try. She had a strength and aura that commanded people's attention and respect. For a significant part of my childhood, I thought people were afraid of her. I was wrong. People respected her. People wanted to meet her and enjoyed being around her. For a woman with little formal education beyond high school, she was the standard for engagement and networking. She commanded the respect of everyone she encountered. I won't be so bold to assert that Mom had no fear. I think that would be disingenuous. I'm sure she experienced being uncertain and nervous in new situations. But she never allowed fear or any emotions remotely associated with it to conquer her mind or her soul. It is that approach that helped prepare me to take on the responsibility of having a career that required me to be able to command the respect of people in the room.

As an Assistant District Attorney for the chief law enforcement agency of Erie County, I did not want to fail. I could not fail. I had no choice. But I carried a responsibility my white colleagues could not understand. Personally, I feared failure and embarrassment. Most importantly, I didn't want to be an embarrassment to my family or to the local black community. It was a challenge every day to stand out positively while remaining true to what I believed. I was routinely tested. In 1995, I was the only black Assistant District Attorney. I dare not fail when the spotlight is bright. Every day, my competence and confidence would be tested. I knew people would take note of every word spoken from my mouth, every plea deal I would make, and assess my ability to comprehend and correctly apply the law. I studied. The standards I set for myself were always higher than anything anyone else could possibly expect. Ironically, I used the fear of failure as a source of motivation to get me through those five and a half to six years. Each and every morning, there were new waters to test. I learned quickly that I was a target for defense attorneys. My first year, a few judges allowed me to learn the hard way from mistakes attributed to my inexperience. I became increasingly motivated and determined to improve my performance every day. I never lost belief or confidence in my abilities and where God positioned me. As Mom maintained her dignity and self-respect, so would I.

The criminal justice system is a world that does not always embrace the presence and influence of black faces. The system is one where a disproportionate number of its offenders are people of color and the authorities are overwhelmingly white. I never intended to choose a career related to criminal prosecution/law enforcement. As I would soon discover, some careers choose you. My first week on the job, I shadowed an Assistant District Attorney who was primarily responsible for prosecuting juveniles. She showed me the ropes and introduced me to people who would be instrumental in helping me understand the juvenile justice system. The personnel in the county's juvenile delinquency department were welcoming and provided assistance whenever I needed it. Within a week or two, I began handling delinquency hearings. On more than one occasion, I was mistaken for the parent of an offender, a public defender, or a new probation officer by the parents and their children.

As black parents became increasingly aware of the new black prosecutor responsible for their child's case, probation officers would tell me, "Elvage, the word is out on you." I became the subject of talk on the street and the county courthouse. There were times when I would attempt to speak with kids checking in with their probation officer. They would tell their friends, "Man, don't talk to him; he's 5-O." Admittedly, I was taken aback by the comments of a child telling his friend not to speak with me. I never recall not listening to a black adult who took the time to address me or who may have had something meaningful to say to me when I was growing up. These black boys could not reconcile how a black male professional might be legitimately concerned about their future while being able to do his job.

After working in juvenile court for less than a year, I was promoted and assigned cases in adult criminal court. Our staff meetings were convened on Friday afternoons. Meetings were comprised of all assistant district attorneys, county detectives, and an administrative assistant. We would receive case law updates, be advised of new policies, and community initiatives pertinent to our roles. In addition, we also staffed homicide cases. This involved reviewing the available evidence, determining if additional investigation was warranted, making charging decisions, and, in some cases, determining whether the death penalty would be sought. During one particular staff meeting, there was a staffing for an unsolved homicide case. This was limited to the attorneys and county detectives. Erie County was the venue for this unsolved homicide. The body of the deceased was dumped in nearby Ohio. The Chief of Police from Ohio, where the body was discovered, was invited to attend the staffing. While listening to the presentation, the chief was discussing how he felt when someone with whom he had come into contact had disrespected him.

While describing the encounter, I heard him say, "He was treating me like I was a black person or something." As offended as I was at that moment, I did not say anything. The staffing continued. I looked around the room at my colleagues, and no one blinked an eye. I was not surprised. Initially, I was very disappointed. At the conclusion of the staff meeting, a few assistant district attorneys remained in the conference room following the meeting, and I asked if they heard the remark made by the police chief. One of my senior colleagues acknowledged hearing the remark and demonstrated his disgust for it. From that moment, I knew the importance of my role and presence in that office. I had already been advised by a number of people within the black community that my presence as an Assistant District Attorney was critical and vital to ensuring justice. In fact, an investigator who worked in the county's public defender office said, "Having you in that office represents us, our concerns and provides a presence and a voice that has been lacking." It was an expectation I took seriously. A second senior Assistant District Attorney told me, "Elvage, I can see how much the environment has noticeably changed in that conference room and challenged the attitudes and language previously used by some in the office since you have been hired." It was no secret that some people didn't want to see me in that position. Some police officers openly expressed doubt in my commitment to vigorously prosecute their cases. What they obviously meant was would I have the commitment to prosecute the black defendants? What many soon discovered was that I was an equal opportunity prosecutor. My duty to seek justice applied universally. I am not going to say I didn't see color or socio-economic status in the offenders. I did. I was not going to leave any doubt about what I stood for, and worked to ensure, justice for all people. If the circumstances of a criminal case and the law determined a white offender was going to get a favorable deal, a similarly situated black offender would get the same plea deal. I refused to submit to the opinions of others. I had a job to do, and I was committed to it. People had no idea of the standard to which I held myself. I was motivated to honor my family in all things. Doing anything else was unacceptable.

Soon after my appointment as a prosecutor, I became aware of the criticism emanating from the communities who were at odds with the Office of the District Attorney. My first week on the job, there was a homicide. The tension and hostility between the black community and the local law enforcement community was high. I began to wonder if I was hired to somehow appease the black community. The one thing white people should know is the hiring of one black prosecutor was not going to cure the longstanding division and mistrust. Although I didn't view myself as a token hire, I knew some would. It was the reality of becoming a part of a community where the professional opportunities for African Americans were negligible. In 1995, the number of African American professionals in Erie was a rarity. In the year I went to law school, Erie County had two black attorneys. Five years later, my move to Erie kept that number at two.

For those professional black men and women who did exist, many worked in public service. Very few owned their own businesses. As I became immersed in my duties, I was getting to know the other county government workers. Some were quick to advise me to stay away from particular black employees and ministers. Others were quick to tell me stories about the failed careers of other black professionals (e.g. lawyers, probation officers, etc.), how they were cut short or quietly reassigned due to addictions and other vices they could not manage.

My first few years in Erie, I would be routinely reminded by white employees of a host of incidents resulting in these black professionals (predominantly men) succumbing to various temptations and never recovering their standing or reputation. What was disconcerting to me is that these individuals had become these beloved caricatures who remain the butt of jokes and ridicule. I always believed some of the same people were expecting me to suffer a similar fall from grace. Why not? That's the way it's been for other black professionals. Then came the unexpected advice I received from an older black woman I met outside the Erie County Court House in 1995. It was a strange encounter. There was no introduction. I always refer to her as my guardian angel. She knew I worked at the courthouse. She approached me and asked, "Are you married? Do you have a family?" I said, "Yes." She replied, "Make sure you go home to your family at night." She turned and walked away. She never said another word. Those words and the way she spoke them penetrated my heart. They were the words only a mother could speak. They were words that conveyed knowledge and wisdom. They instilled a fear that helped me to be mindful and to take the actions necessary to fulfill my personal and professional obligations. I don't recall ever seeing this woman again. I remembered her advice. I went home every night to my family for the next twenty-three years while living in Erie.

Chapter VII

The Fight for Justice is a Partnership

There is no greater obstacle to a criminal case than a non-cooperating material witness who is capable, yet refuses to come forward and provide truthful information. People may not want to get involved in a matter due to the social or financial costs associated with it. It may present an inconvenience, or result in lost time, wages, etc., that cannot be recouped. When compared to a community's need for truth and inevitably justice, an inconvenience, no matter how significant it appears, pales in comparison to the family and communities harmed by silence. Such rationale is not always sufficient to convince people to set aside their fear to publicly step forward and provide truthful testimony, especially against the backdrop of a "stop snitching" culture, which discourages and threatens witnesses and victims of crime. When fear induces and compels the adoption of a belief that truth should no longer be revered or disclosed for the sole purpose of achieving a perverted sense of justice, the foundation and hope for prosperity is ripped away.

Those who are viewed as the essential players in the search for truth and justice are often viewed and treated as a means to an end. If people are not valued or respected, and made invisible to those to whom such authority and power are entrusted, they are not likely to yield and respond to a request for assistance. This is a common reaction I received from victims and witnesses whose cooperation I required to successfully prosecute criminal cases. They would be quick to remind me, "You don't live in my neighborhood. All you care about is your case." They were correct in both instances. But I wanted justice, and I wanted them to want it for themselves and their communities. Admittedly, I struggled to respond to many of these issues and concerns. Nevertheless, I had hoped what we had in common would help bridge the divide. Tapping into shared concerns and cultivating relationships helped open the lines of communication. I had success and continued to make progress in areas I would not have otherwise thought possible.

There were moments when cases were assigned to me in the hope that I might be able to better connect with members of the African American community. Although it was not publicly acknowledged within the prosecutor's office, I believed the assignment of a case file for trial was presented to me because my race coincided with the race of the victims and witnesses. Initially, I recall being offended. I prepared and presented these cases for trial. After taking a moment to think about the dynamics of these cases objectively, I recognized that it presented an opportunity. I was committed to engaging and listening to the grievances of the black citizens in our community. I thought maybe I could cultivate relationships and help build a bridge between the black community and the Office of the District Attorney that could be sustained indefinitely. It would not come without understanding and acknowledging the history of a city and county where people of color have been historically excised from the policy-making process.

Trust had to be built. An olive branch needed to be extended. I was not a product of Erie. My family was not from this town. The people in positions of power and authority did not make it easier. There were some white people who were kind enough and correct to tell me to be mindful of black people who could not be trusted and that there would be black people who would be threatened by my presence and who would not hesitate to hurt me if he or she felt it was necessary for their survival and prosperity. The "crab mentality" was alive and well in Erie. There were some white people who did everything they could to tell me how I better think and what to believe. Some went so far as to try and define the scope of my relationships and affiliations. In addition, I received warnings from Erieites about local politicians, business owners, and ministers who took advantage of others.

With the support of my wife, we decided to be different. We knew trust is built on being givers, not takers. We gave of ourselves in every way imaginable. We invested our time and money into initiatives and relationships that did not come without sacrifices and loss to our own family. Yet, it did prove to be successful. Bridges were built with those who only saw the police and the court systems as the enemy. Absent relationships, you don't have a foothold to meet people where they are to convince them to come forward and make the necessary sacrifice to reveal what they know to ensure justice.

My career as an attorney was always premised on the belief in truth and justice. It was not lip service. People clamor for justice. Yet, they don't want to do anything about it until it's forced upon them. George Floyd's death (2020) resulted from the conduct of a rogue Minneapolis police officer. The protest and riots ensued throughout the country. Rightfully so, we demanded justice for George Floyd and his family. When the righteousness of justice is delayed or denied, people become enraged. Justice should be an immediate expectation, universally established and imposed without delay. If an injustice occurs in one case, it becomes like a virus and spreads. Over time, we get used to behaving and accepting those things that allow injustices to take place before our eyes. It's a product of the fear and silence that we allow to abide in us.

When the death of George Floyd occurred, there was a collective angst. We were ready to confront and challenge armed police officers and members of the National Guard. But we need to exhibit this same righteous indignation for any crime to which we might have information relating to the identity and location of offenders who must be arrested and criminally prosecuted. The word "snitch" should be treated like the slurs and other derogatory words used to marginalize and oppress black people. It should be reclaimed, converted into an acronym viewed as a mechanism by which we *See the Need to Intervene, Tell, and Call for Help*. The word "snitch" has, and will, continue to polarize our communities until it is reclaimed. It is used, and relied on, by those who seek to hold immeasurable power over another person. The use and allegiance to this term in its current form releases people from the responsibility of looking out for another person. It has people living within a vacuum and taking no ownership of their communities. Simply, justice calls for us to do the right thing every time. Justice calls for us to do what is difficult and hard. Justice always requires sacrifice, commitment, and placing the needs of others before our own. If we are ever to expect true justice to be realized in the performance of police officers and prosecutors, it begins with the small steps we are required to take to ensure that justice is meted out in our own families. Moments will most certainly arise that will test our allegiances to our communities and nation. In all likelihood, this testing will take place outside of the public eye. The results may not provide you with public acclaim or a reward; though it may have the effect of saving the life of someone who is under your care and ultimately define your character.

What I am calling for requires a dramatic paradigm shift. It may require breaking allegiances and exhibiting tough love. The fruit of justice must be exhibited universally before it can be universally expected. We must be prepared to take a stand. Little did I know a test to do the same awaited our family.

In August 2008, our son, James, enrolled in college at the campus where I was employed. His transition was less than successful. Simply, he had an inauspicious beginning to his college career. About midway through his first semester, I received a phone call from Janel advising me she had been made aware of the possibility that our son was in possession of a firearm based on a picture he posted to social media. She said, "I just saw his Facebook page. He is pictured posing with and holding a gun. I don't know if it's real or fake. It looks real." After she told me that he was depicted brandishing it in an ominous manner, I said, "I will look into it." I was in a precarious position. I was a faculty member at the same university and the father of a student who may or may not have been in possession of a gun. In addition, the April 2007 mass shooting at Virginia Tech University was still fresh in my mind. It was all I could think about. Thirty-three people were tragically killed at Virginia Tech. I had never experienced being angry, frightened, and wanting to protect my son at the same time. I was obviously conflicted between my love for him and the impact of this matter on his life, and my responsibilities to the welfare of the university community. I knew it wasn't anything

I could casually ignore and pass off as inconsequential. In addition, I knew by making a decision to contact authorities, it had the potential of causing a permanent divide within our family. There was no easy out. Other than Janel, who else could I call for advice? To the best of my knowledge, there wasn't time for that. What do I do? *Do I go to his dorm room? Do I try to track him down based on his class schedule or contact his professors and instructors to see if he is in class?* I thought, *That will not work; he is an adult!* In addition, I could not abandon my own professional responsibilities at that moment. I knew I had to do something. For over six years, I had become a trusted member of the university's faculty. I had developed relationships with students and faculty, earned their respect, and knew my responsibilities to each and every person within our university community. My no-nonsense belief in always doing the right thing was being tested. *Would I pass this test?* I have witnessed and criticized parents for coming to the rescue of their adult children who have committed heinous crimes. Now, I was facing a similar dilemma. All I could think about was how this situation ended up on our family's threshold. All I could do was bow my head in prayer. I asked God, "Lord, grant me Your guidance and direction." After what felt like an entirety, I knew what I had to do. I contacted Janel and told her what steps I was going to take. She agreed.

I contacted a university administrator and explained to him what my wife had seen. He told me, "I will contact the university police and have them conduct a check at his dorm room." He said, "I will contact you and let you know when we know something for certain." An officer was dispatched to his living community.

After the officer arrived, she walked to the outside window of his first-floor room and saw what appeared to be a firearm situated on the windowsill. The officer proceeded to knock on the door. James answered the door and allowed them to enter his room. When they advised him that they had a report of a gun being kept in his room, he directed them to what appeared to be a 9 MM Glock sitting on the windowsill. Upon their inspection of the firearm, it was determined to be an air pistol. He had recently purchased it. The matter was reported to university officials, and soon thereafter, our son was told to pack up and leave campus immediately. He called Janel and advised her of what happened. He gathered the items he could and took refuge a few miles from campus, where I picked him up a few hours later. I was numb. When I laid eyes on him, I did not give him a fatherly embrace. However, I was relieved he was safe and that nothing tragic came from it. The burden I felt like I was carrying to protect my university community dissipated. I had a brief conversation with him about what he was going to do next. I told him, "Before you are allowed to return home, you are going to go to your summer employer this afternoon and get back on a full-time work schedule. In addition, tomorrow you are going to see the United States Air Force Recruiter." Once he agreed to those conditions, he picked up his belongings, and I took him home. In short, he fulfilled both conditions. It was a very challenging time for our family. The variability of emotions in our household that night, and over the next few days, ranged from anger, rage, sadness, embarrassment, disappointment, and resentment. After he had been home for less than an hour, something within me snapped. My son stood at 6'4". I am 5'8". As we were standing in the garage having it out about having a gun and his so-called gang affiliation, I told him, "If you are such a tough guy, fight me! Fight me!" I did everything I could to start a fight. He wouldn't engage me. He said, "I don't fight." I was so angry

I picked him up, and raised him over my head and threw him to the ground. He looked up at me with fear in his eyes. When I looked up a Pennsylvania State Trooper vehicle was slowly passing in front of our home. Whether the Trooper(s) witnessed what transpired, I have no idea. I went into the house, walked upstairs and received something from my wife and daughter I did not expect to receive. They were cheering me on. I recall my wife saying, "That's what he needed." I was surprised by her support. James is the first born—her baby. Yet, I was relieved to receive it.

There was no second-guessing the actions Janel and I agreed to take regarding our son, and why. Thirteen years later, we would have taken the same action. While living and working in Erie, I saw the result of what happened to young people who were enabled and not held accountable by members of their own families. I was not going to lose our son to the temptation of the streets that had taken countless young lives. My wife and I are convinced that our desire to remain aligned with truth, and ensuring justice for all people regardless of the public embarrassment or humiliation we may have endured, saved our son in more ways than we could possibly imagine. He is with us today because we were able to put aside and not allow the fear of him being arrested, criminally prosecuted, or going to jail prevent us from doing the right thing. In addition, we are blessed to have a strong relationship with our son, James. He has persevered and has learned how his behavior has consequences. He attributes the quality and appreciation for his life to the difficult actions his parents were compelled to take. Justice is a partnership. Justice requires taking ownership (responsibility) of a matter and acknowledging one's actions or obligation (accountability). We did the former. Our son did the latter.

We didn't ask or expect a particular outcome regarding the university's disciplinary action. However, I believe the actions we agreed to take that day in November 2008 helped mitigate the damage and the penalty he received, if the conduct in question had been discovered independent of our *Seeing the Need to Intervene, Tell, and Call for Help*.

Chapter VIII

All They See is This...

Prior to my arrival in Erie, there was a noticeable divide between the City of Erie's police department and the African American community. The black community did not trust or respect the local law enforcement community. My understanding of these issues was one of the many reasons I shied away from the prospect of becoming a prosecutor after graduating from law school. The lack of representation of people of color in police departments and in courthouse operations was readily apparent in Erie. I had hoped my presence and work within the criminal justice system would inspire hope and confidence among the African American community that the criminal justice system can work to our benefit, not just to our detriment. But the reality of how I was viewed was realized the first day I walked into a courtroom to observe a colleague prosecute a criminal case. My participation was as his co-counsel. Thus, my role was limited. I was astounded by the reaction of representatives of the juvenile probation department, parents, children, opposing counsel, and police officers upon realizing I would be serving as a prosecutor in Erie County. The questions ranged from "Who is he?" to "Who is his family? How did he get in the District Attorneys office?"

To some, my hire was unconventional and a political gimmick. Within the first month on the job, I received lunch invitations from a few judges, who said they were interested in welcoming me to the community, and they did. A few were more concerned about impressing upon me how fair they are perceived and how highly regarded they are by the black community. There were rumors among the defense bar that my appointment was nothing more than an attempt by the outgoing and incoming District Attorney to curry favors with the leadership within the African American community. It was remarkable how bold people were about expressing their opinions and thoughts on my hiring. Regardless of the motives or rationale behind my hiring, it did little to help ease my transition. I knew the opportunity before me was an important one. I had to fulfill my responsibilities in a way that would bring honor to the African American community and help instill a new level of confidence in its local justice system. I was determined to not embarrass the black community.

Approximately six months after my hiring, I began transitioning out of juvenile court, and making more appearances in adult criminal court. My presence was noticeable. At the time of my hire, the O.J. Simpson trial was at the tail end of concluding. A few members of the local defense bar would jokingly refer to me as "Chris Darden." Usually, it was in response to me standing my ground and vehemently disagreeing with their arguments. When it did happen, I said, "Thank you for the compliment." I knew the intention of the reference was not a compliment. The derogatory references would continue. I would endure them. No matter how familiar and accomplished I had become in my capacity as a prosecutor, there were moments when the negative perceptions to which so many in this community comfortably accepted about people of color would often be directed toward me. There was no escaping or avoiding the stereotypes people would attempt to assign to me. It was inevitable. Little did "they" know, my parents prepared me to rise above the narrow-minded and preconceived opinions of those I would encounter.

In 1994, before my appointment as a prosecutor, I had a scheduled appearance before a county judge. I was representing a client who had been charged with a speeding violation. Prior to my arrival, I spoke with the prosecutor (who later became the District Attorney for this particular county) and worked out an agreement to allow my client to enter a plea of guilty to traveling at a reduced speed. I walked in with my client who is white. We were both dressed in suits. We took our position at the defense table. I took the position traditionally reserved for the attorney. The prosecutor did the same. As the judge entered the courtroom, all parties and the people in the gallery rose to their feet. My case was the first to be called. My client and I remained on our feet. The judge directed the prosecutor to call his first case. The prosecutor advised the judge that an agreement had been reached in our case. The judge looked over to our table, looked at my client, and said, "Is that correct, counselor?" Before I could speak up, my client advised the judge, "I am not the attorney. He is the attorney." At that moment, my parents' voices and lessons were stirring inside of me. I remember thinking to myself, "Here we go." It's just what my parents warned me about. "Elvage, some people will only see this . . ." When my mother or father would say this to me, they would always point at the top of their other hand denoting their skin tone.

My client was charged with a motor vehicle violation that could have resulted in a license suspension if he were convicted of the offense charged. I'm sure my client/friend chalked it up to the judge making a simple mistake. He didn't care about the judge's "mistake." I was hired to do a job. Anything else I may have been feeling and experiencing at that moment was of no consequence to my client and could not interfere with me performing my ethical duty to be his advocate. The reaction and look on the judge's face was memorable. I looked up toward the bench and advised the judge, "Your Honor, we have reached an agreement and Mr. _____ has agreed to enter a plea of guilty to the amended charge." The judge asked my client if he was willing to pay all costs and fines at the conclusion of the matter. He agreed, and the matter ended. I walked out of the courtroom, said goodbye to my client, and left. I traveled a considerable distance to represent a friend, and a judge presumed I was the defendant. But sadly, I was not shocked by the experience. I wasn't remotely surprised by the judge's lack of perspective. I had been prepared for the moment I just experienced. What else could I expect from a judge in a rural county of western Pennsylvania? Was he prejudiced or a bigot? Possibly. Is it possible his interactions with black people were limited to those who were brought before him on criminal charges? Maybe. Is it possible he never had a black attorney make an appearance before him representing a white client? This is more likely. I am fortunate I had parents who prepared me to face people who would be disrespectful or offend my sensibilities. What is impressive about my parents is that they always taught us that not every white person you encounter is prejudiced, a bigot, or racist.

I have walked into a lot of courthouses and courtrooms throughout the Commonwealth of Pennsylvania. No matter how long I practiced and how well dressed I was when making a formal appearance, these "mistakes" did not end. There was a time when a defense attorney presumed I was the client he was waiting on to arrive. On another occasion, a sheriff's deputy mistakenly believed I was a defendant scheduled to enter a plea or to be sentenced. Although these mistakes were short-lived, it was a reminder that there were people who were not accustomed to seeing a person of color in any other capacity other than as a criminal defendant. It was a burden I would have to endure. It was my responsibility to force people to set aside such biases based on my performances and how I represented myself. There was no time to allow the discomfort of being offended by a remark or a person's poor judgment to excuse me from performing the duties associated with the oath or responsibilities I had taken.

Every court or public appearance presented an "opportunity," whether I liked it or not, to demonstrate that black people are not limited to the roles envisioned by those who saw us predominantly as criminal defendants or people who should be grateful for what white people are willing to give us. There are people in this world who just don't know black people or anything about us other than what they choose to believe. Mom and Dad encouraged us to listen to white people, think about the scope of their experiences with black people, or the lack thereof, and be willing to teach, enlighten, and forgive white people when there is a true demonstration of contrition for acts of bigotry, racism, or discrimination. An opportunity to forgive someone presented itself when I received the following email on April 17, 2018:

Subject: Hello and Please Forgive Me

Date: Monday, April 16, 2018 . . .

From: [PC]

To: Murphy, Elvage

Dear Elvage (. . .)

I don't know if you remember me, but you and I were friends during our freshmen year at Edinboro in 1983. We lived on opposite sides of the same floor in Rose Hall.

I have many fond memories of you and of that year in particular. However, throughout the years since, I've carried with me one memory that I've always regretted. It's stayed with me for 35 years now and I am as ashamed today of my behavior towards you as I was on the day that it took place. This is why I'm writing to you now.

For me, the details are still so very clear. My heart aches and I've endured the exact same degree of shame and embarrassment each time that I've remembered or reflected upon that one particular day. If you don't recall the incident, here's what happened. Several of us were in one of the guy's rooms joking around and basically hanging out. You were the only black guy there, which wasn't of any consequence, at least to me or so I believed. As I mentioned, we were friends and race had never been an issue between us. Anyway, I was excusing myself from the group when I said, "Yeah, I gotta get up early and go listen to a lecture from some n____[r] heart surgeon tomorrow."

A prominent Africa-American surgeon was speaking on campus the next day. I don't remember the doctor's name or even who he was. What I do remember was the immediate sickening feeling that overcame me as I realized that you were in the room and then I left; knowing full well what a vile disgusting thing I had just said and done. I went to my room and began to repent, first for what I thought at the time to be having hurt or embarrassed you, then in my 18 year old mind at what an ass I had made of myself. Instead of apologizing I chose to try and escape my behavior, ultimately choosing to avoid you for the rest of my time at Edinboro. Please know that shame is what drove my subsequent behavior . . .

. . . I thank God for the coincident and for allowing me an opportunity to extend to you my most sincere apology, Elvage. Along with my apology to you, please know that I have truly tried to educate myself and to understand how my words and actions affect others no matter what the circumstances or situation. . .

If you can find it in your heart to forgive me, I beg you to do so. Also, I pray that one day we may meet so that I may more appropriately apologize in person and perhaps rekindle our friendship.

Admittedly, I don't recall the incident with the same degree of specificity he describes. I read his email a few times. My wife and children have read it. I cannot imagine a person carrying a burden for thirty-five years and needing to seek out forgiveness for it. It was apparent that his need for forgiveness outweighed any pain his remark may have caused me. I responded to the email and granted him the forgiveness he requested. I hope he has the peace he needs to direct his energy and attention to his family and career. He assured me that he shares this horrible memory with anyone he can to illustrate the ugliness of his ignorance and the potential harm it may cause.

Listening, teaching, and forgiving white people are not burdens I am eager to carry. Yet, it remains a responsibility I will continue to fulfill. I want to ensure the blessings of liberty for me, and my family. Thus, I must demand more of myself as a citizen, in order to compel others to do the same.

Chapter IX

It's Not Personal

Growing up predominantly in the 1970s and 80s, discussions about instances of injustice and discrimination were common at my church, social settings with friends and family, barbershops, beautician parlors, etc. These discussions occurred in places frequented by black people and outside the purview of white counsel. I know that is the reason why I have such a high regard for justice and equality and was inspired to become a lawyer. I was always quick to identify when I thought something was wrong, even if I didn't know why.

According to Aristotle, "The law is reason free from passion."[1] The law is the mechanism by which we look into something and allow rules to guide and direct us to arrive at a decision based on the factual information presented. It's the reason by which we arrive at a conclusion without being influenced by our emotions. But there were more than a few occasions when I allowed my passion for truth and justice, and the need to protect others, to overcome that reason.

---

1. Aristotle

In 1996, I was assigned the responsibility to prosecute individuals charged with indirect criminal contempt for violating protection from abuse orders against their spouses or significant others. For approximately a month, one man's name (hereinafter referred to as I.R.) had become an increasingly familiar one on the docket every week. It was not out of the ordinary for putative victims to contact the office the week before the scheduled contempt hearing, expressing their desire to cease the prosecution. I would be advised they were not going to appear in court, and to withdraw the protective order. It was standard practice for a case to be dismissed when a victim/witness did not appear, or requested to have the order withdrawn, unless a continuance and rescheduling of the hearing was granted. Finally, I had enough of I.R.'s cases being dismissed. The next phone call I received from his complainant, I advised her that if she wanted to have the case dismissed, she would be required to come to court, be sworn in, stand before the judge, and express her desire to cease the prosecution. She did, and the judge entered a court order to have the case dismissed. At the conclusion of the proceeding, the defendant was walking out of the courtroom smiling and boasting to his friend, "I got off." I followed up and made sure I conveyed a message to him he would never forget. I was noticeably upset. One of my colleagues felt it was necessary to grab me and guide me back to our office. Was my frustration and anger with this particular perpetrator justified? I thought so at the time.

In 1997, I appeared at a sentencing hearing following the successful prosecution of a man for sexually abusing his biological daughter. The victim and her mother were present. At the conclusion of the sentencing hearing, the defendant's brother uttered a racial epithet and a few other choice expletives at me as he walked quickly out of the courtroom.

I followed him and we had a brief exchange of words in the hallway. Unbeknownst to me, the judge heard, or became aware of, the argument in the hallway. After some time had passed, the judge contacted me and asked me to come to his chambers. Upon my arrival, he immediately began to share his disappointment in the way I had handled myself in the hallway. He said it was reminiscent to how people behave on the street. He was right. I knew it. Again, what did it accomplish?

In both instances, the behavior I exhibited fell far below what most reasonable people would expect from someone who is entrusted with a public position of authority and power. Most importantly, I succumbed to the instinct and anger I was experiencing at the time. In both situations, I allowed my sensibilities to be offended and controlled by the conduct and words of strangers. For a brief moment, I gave them ownership over my heart and mind. I forfeited a peace neither person could give me. I made it personal.

As a child, and into my younger adult years, I was sensitive to losing and criticism. It was rare when it happened. When it did, it stung. My brother and I were loved. But I cannot say we were nurtured like other children. I remember being raised to work hard and become a successful adult. When I embarked upon my career, a perfect performance was my standard. Making mistakes and missing the mark was, and is, not acceptable to me. I viewed it as a personal affront to my competence and commitment. My father would remind me how important it is to receive all criticism, whether you like it or not. My mother would encourage me to see it as a test of your maturity and strength. Both are credited for helping me to see I cannot afford to take any encounter personally. Our parents were always ahead of the curve when it came to preparing us for criticism and insults. Mom was always preaching about not allowing the things people say to get to you. She would say, "You have to ignore them. They don't know anything about you or your family." Dad would say, "Don't take it personally; its business." Both would have been very disappointed that I allowed two strangers to get into my head and cause me to react in a fashion that would place myself in a compromising position. Mom would say, "Boy! Don't you know you have too much to lose. People who behave that way are trying to bring you down to their level. You have to be better. Nobody is going to feel sorry for you. People are likely to view it as a sign of weakness if you cannot maintain your composure." I realized that these moments are designed to shine a brighter light on black people and determine if we are who we claim to be. I had to make a decision. Do I take comfort in the array of emotions generated by being offended, or do I choose to rise above it and respond in a way that is consistent with my professional mandate to fight for justice and ensure peace?

In both of those courthouse encounters, I abandoned self-control and my common sense. I later realized that I chose to be offended. The offensive conduct of these two men stung, albeit momentarily. I surrendered to it. My frustration and willingness to be confrontational with both men were instantaneous and driven by my ego. No matter my rationalization, the emotional reactions to having been offended yielded nothing of substance. Both men left the courthouse, and I never laid eyes on either one again. I was left with the stares and recollections of courthouse employees and former colleagues who share exaggerated tales of what they remembered seeing.

 I had to realize that we do control the extent to which we may allow the offensive conduct of another to violate the parameters and quality of our lives. According to Roberta Cava, "You can't control other people's behavi[or], but you can control your responses to it."[2] This very popular phrase showcases the need for us to recognize that we do, and must, exercise stewardship over our temperament and conduct when responding to unpleasant people and offensive remarks, etc.

> No one can make you feel any negative emotion—fear, anger, or inferiority—without your express permission. There will always be people who find perverse enjoyment in upsetting others, or who simply play upon your emotions so that they can use you for their own selfish purposes. Whether or not they are successful depends entirely upon you and how you react to their negative behaviors. When you are forced to deal with such people, recognize from the outset that they are trying to upset you, not because of something you may have done to them, but because of some problem they have with themselves. Tell yourself, "This isn't about me. I will not allow this person to upset me. I am in control of my emotions and my life.[3]

My parents preached a similar message to us over and over again. Only after being married over twenty-five years and raising two children am I now able to live it out consistently. I have known people who are unwilling to see beyond the hurt and pain they attribute to others. Simply, they will not let go. I would ask friends, "Is it more important for you to be right or to have peace?" Typically, and understandably, the response is, "But you don't know what they did to me." How could I possibly argue this point? They were correct. I could not appreciate

---

2. Cava, Roberta, Dealing with difficult people: How to deal with nasty customers, demanding bosses and uncooperative colleagues. (2008)

3. Quote attributed to the The Napoleon Hill Foundation, Thought for the Day, 4/18, 2017; www.naphill.org

their experience. They could not possibly appreciate mine. The pain and resentment they were experiencing was undeniable and was still being processed. The time was not ripe for reconciliation. They remained fixated on the conduct of the offender, rather than focusing on acquiring the skills to manage their pain and transcend the anger and bitterness for the peace that awaited them. They were not ready to forgive the offender. According to Marianne Williamson, "Unforgiveness is like drinking poison yourself and waiting for the other person to die." Most reasonable people do not intentionally ingest poison. Poison produces adverse effects on people and a variety of symptoms, like a headache or nausea, may manifest and potentially lead to more severe symptoms causing irreparable damage. The ingestion of poison requires medical treatment and hospitalization to offset its potential effects. If the effect of holding on to the anger and resentment one attributes to being offended is analogous to poison, it is important to realize there is an antidote at our disposal if we desire to use it. Submitting to proper treatment is a necessary component of our response. Allowing the remnant of an offense to remain and take up permanent residency is an obstacle to the peace that is considerably more valuable than the apology one believes he or she is entitled to receive from their offender.

Offenses may arrive unexpectedly and abruptly. Some are more egregious than others and will remain a part of our lives longer than they should if we allow it. They test our maturity and ability to appropriately navigate and manage the emotions they provoke. The ultimate test of my maturity came while I was campaigning for judge in 2015.

On the day of the primary election, I was standing in front of a polling place in Millcreek Township speaking with a prospective supporter.

I greeted and attempted to introduce myself to an elderly white man who was entering the polling place. As I extended my hand, he would not reciprocate the gesture and gave me a searing glance as he walked into the polling place.

The encounters and people I experienced throughout the campaign offended my notions of common courtesy and respect. You name it. Each situation left an indelible mark that is impossible to eliminate from my memory. I never received an apology from those who offended me. I never forgot the circumstances of those situations. Nonetheless, I realized the offended person is entrusted with the responsibility of deciding the extent of an offense's impact. I could not afford to yield to the anger and resentment I experienced during those moments. A judicial campaign needed to be completed.

In order to remain a viable judicial candidate, it was important that I exhibit the temperament and professionalism required to serve as a judge. A white female supporter, who was present, witnessed the interaction between me, and the prospective voter. She watched intently how I responded. I recalled telling the gentlemen, "Have a nice day, sir," as he entered the polling place. I continued to introduce myself to other voters as they entered and thanked others for their support. Making oneself available for public office should test and reveal our character when faced with opposition, resistance, and outright rejection. I would not allow the conduct of one person to tear away at the foundation of my campaign. Honoring the community and my family was more important than the sting of the offensive conduct of one man that I endured at an inopportune moment.

Chapter X

Own it!

Throughout my legal career, in particular, in criminal cases, I have had some interesting discussions with former clients. I recall discussions with former clients who would advise me they did not believe they did anything wrong because their actual conduct was not the same as the conduct of a co-conspirator. In one situation, a former client tried to argue he was not guilty and could get off on charges of robbery and criminal conspiracy to commit robbery since he did not enter the store or possess the gun. According to him, all he agreed to do was drive his friend to a store. Yet, he knew the friend was armed and what he was going to do after he entered the store. Following the commission of the robbery, the gunman returned to the car, at which time my client admitted asking the gunman for some of the candy taken during the commission of the crime. He argued that he should not have been charged with any crimes or have to go to jail because, in his mind, all he did was pick up, drive, drop off, and pick up his friend again. After I explained the concepts and legal elements of accomplice liability and conspiracy, he began to understand and accept that his involvement, albeit different from that of his co-conspirator, put him on the same legal footing as his co-conspirator. Nonetheless, he continued to assert that the manner in which his case was being prosecuted was unfair. Although my former client's rationale was incorrect, it was an all-too-common position that I would grow accustomed to hearing and observing. I would commonly refer to it as the "art of deflection."

Deflection is designed to blame others and distract people from focusing on truth. In America, we have become experts in deflection and passed it down to our nation's posterity. This is not what the founders of *The Preamble* envisioned. Deflection shifts the blame for our inadequacies and failures to others, all in an effort to avoid responsibility. It is as American as apple pie. All my life, my parents and family made certain we were aware of the injustices experienced by black people and the steps some white people took to contribute to the systemic oppression and discrimination of black people. The hopes, dreams, and work of black people have been denied, stolen, and often to the financial benefit of some white people. These discussions were a reminder that racism and discrimination were alive and well and should be expected. Yet, Dad and Mom balanced this truth with another: "Do not use racism as an excuse for not doing your work. Do not use racism as an excuse for your failure. You have no excuses. I don't ever want to hear you using white people as an excuse for failure." This was a delicate balance to maintain. My parents' and grandparents' generations endured much greater obstacles than I could ever imagine. They did a great job of helping us to walk a tightrope intertwined with facts and logic. We learned that every unfavorable outcome didn't necessarily equate to an act of racism and discrimination. Living up to this expectation was challenging, especially when you become astute at recognizing a true pretext for racism that has a discriminatory impact. Dad and Mom set a tone that positioned us to see the reality of a world filled with racism without succumbing to the hands of its perpetrators and, most importantly, to deflection.

Employing deflection negates the need to take responsibility or ownership of a dilemma or situation. Deflection leaves no appreciation for truth. If there is no appreciation for truth, we will not establish a foundation to prepare future generations to effectively navigate life's challenges as they arise. "[T]oo many of today's children have straight teeth and crooked morals."[1] We operate with the misplaced belief that, just because young people are clean, presentable, and well-dressed, that somehow they are beyond submitting to the propensity to deflect away the responsibility associated with their conduct.

When I began my legal career as a prosecutor in 1995, it didn't take me long to learn that many of the kids and teenagers I would encounter were operating under a state of moral confusion from which many would be hard-pressed to distance themselves without someone to lead them. Juveniles ranged between ten to seventeen years of age. Some remained under the supervision of the juvenile court system until the time they were twenty-one years of age. In some cases, a team comprised of probation officers, a juvenile court hearing master, a supervising county judge, and treatment officials would stand in *loco parentis*, in the place of a parent, until such time the juvenile reached majority or was permanently discharged from the jurisdiction of the juvenile system. These children came into contact with these authorities more than the biological members of their families. In many cases, representatives of the criminal justice and juvenile

---

1. Feazel and Swain citing to remarks of an unidentified high school principal, pg. 178

justice systems became family to these juveniles. Watching children attend hearings without parents or guardians was disturbing. It was commonplace to see children accompanied by their assigned probation officer and an arresting police officer testifying to justify their detention for allegedly committing acts of delinquency. When parents did appear at the time of their child's scheduled hearing, many were agitated and often became argumentative and combative about the legitimacy of their child's arrest or detention.

In one particular situation, two police officers entered my office on an early Wednesday morning to consult with me about an arrest they made. They stopped, detained, and searched a fifteen-year-old male who was out on the street that same Wednesday morning at or around 1:00 a.m. After the officers conducted a search of his person, they removed a large amount of crack cocaine from his pocket. The amount was so significant that, if he had been an adult, he would have been facing a mandatory minimum sentence if convicted in adult criminal court. The amount recovered was not consistent with personal use. It was an amount consistent with the intent to deliver or sell. The mother of the juvenile showed for the hearing. She was understandably upset. But her anger and disappointment were not directed toward her son. She was upset with the police officers for detaining and searching her son. She yelled repeatedly at both officers and called them names. Before she arrived for her son's hearing, the juvenile was calm, amiable with his assigned defense counsel and cooperative with representatives of the juvenile probation department. In addition, he was in good physical condition. I reviewed the booking sheet. There was no evidence of him being mistreated or physically abused. Admittedly, the stop was questionable. An opportunity would be provided to litigate this issue separately from the request to detain him. What was inescapable the entire time during Mom's rant was her failure to express or direct her anger or dissatisfaction at her son for being arrested with a large amount of crack cocaine on his person or question why he had it or what he was going to do with it. Her rage and frustration were directed exclusively at the officers and the defense attorney assigned to represent her son. You can imagine the nature of the message Mom conveyed to her son by deflecting the responsibility for the stop, search, and his arrest toward the authorities, and not attributing it to her son.

I did not know this mother. I had no knowledge of her background, struggles, and challenges as a parent. There were a number of conclusions I could arrive at about her. One was obvious. This mother was not properly positioned or equipped (for whatever reason) to shield her son from the circumstances he encountered. As I reflect on my upbringing, there is no way either of my parents would have made excuses or allowed their fifteen-year-old sons to be out at 1:00 a.m. There would have been hell to pay. My parents were not only properly positioned to convey words of instruction but were in a position to know and account for our whereabouts at all times. This is how they ensured that we took responsibility and were held accountable for our actions.

My parents' approach was hard. There were times when our excuses and explanations were justified. They refused to entertain them and would often cut us off. Sometimes, it resulted in us getting in trouble for things that were not the creation of our own hands. As our mother would say, "Well, consider it a punishment for something you got away with that I do not know about." The consequences may not have always been fair. Nevertheless, it reinforced a valuable lesson that life is not always fair.

Chapter XI

Our Posterity

From 1995-2017, living and working in Erie provided my wife, Janel, and I with its fair share of challenges. We raised two children. And nothing gives me greater joy than to see both of our children become adults who are capable of managing their lives and rising to face the challenges that our nation and world presents. As I came to discover, parenting, like politics, is not for the faint of heart. Each and every day, my wife and I (like a lot of other parents) were committed to preserving our son and daughter's childhood. We wanted them to have one. This was my wife's primary concern, and I did everything within my ability to honor her. Commitments to having dinner as a family, helping the kids with their homework, praying with them, getting them ready for, and transporting them to school was downright exhausting. Yet, it was our agreement to devote our time and resources to fulfill our moral and legal duty that surpassed our individual and collective needs and interests.

Aside from carrying out our day-to-day responsibilities, we made considerable efforts to make sure our son and daughter were not being exposed to influences that would run counter to our values and what we considered to be important for their well-being and development. As they grew older, their needs for freedom to form their own relationships and test the waters made it very difficult to protect them from the challenges we knew they would experience. Our children were not perfect. They misbehaved and often required some physical correction. We experienced loss and endured disappointments like all families. By the grace of God, we provided what we believed our children needed most: a solid, consistent family structure where they saw the dynamic of a healthy relationship (e.g. communication, cooperation, selflessness, mutual respect, commitment, forgiveness, and love). My wife and I were fortunate. We are products of families that exemplified most of the positive elements of a traditional family. We had a template to follow, and it proved to be a foundation for how we wanted our family to function. Subsequent to our arrival and getting settled in Erie, our kids soon discovered their family was not a *true* reflection of the reality they would see in the lives of their classmates and friends.

Erie exposed our children to households where men were not physically present within the households of their friends. Both James and Heléna quickly learned about the realities of parental absence, and that every child is not a product of a two-parent home with a mother and father. In most situations, they discovered no father was present. I recall a time when a friend of my daughter's came to our home and asked, "Who is that?" My daughter said, "That's my dad." It was difficult to explain to my kids why some kids did not live with their fathers or know their fathers. We did the best we could to help them understand. While being confronted with these circumstances, it also became necessary to consider the emotional toll on our own children and to dispel any notion or fear that I would not return home. This became apparent when I would come home late from work or some community function and be told by my wife, "The kids were asking where's Dad. When is Dad coming home?" According to Janel, they would not go to sleep until I was home, prayed with them, and said, "Goodnight." Thus, it became incumbent upon me to make a conscientious effort to be emotionally available to our children. As they began to understand the home lives of other children, it did provide our family the opportunity to form relationships and extend the scope of our family to include children with whom our son and daughter became acquainted.

Being an interracial family brought its own set of challenges. Before my wife and I married, we discussed the issues related to raising children. I remember when I gave my opinion on how I believed children who are a product of black and white parents should be raised. I told her, "I want to raise our kids to identify as black." Growing up in the black community, I was raised to believe that, if a person had a single drop of black blood, they are black. This was not a rule of the black community. This was the rule of law established in many states that promoted Jim Crow segregation. This was a standard created during the institution of slavery and remains its legacy. My future wife was taken a back by this position. It was something she never heard before. She said, "What about their white side or my family?" As our discussion continued, I said, "Raising bi-racial children to adopt a black identity will help them grow to love who they are and how God made them." I continued to explained to her that, "When children from mixed parentage are out in public, the first thing people will see is this (pointing to my skin and denoting my darker tone)." I asked her, "Do you really think people are going to take the time to think, maybe he or she has a white parent? All black children, regardless of the variation of their skin tone need to be equipped with an appreciation and love of how they look. I want our kids to see the beauty in their skin color and not feel shamed or inadequate when someone makes a disparaging comment about them or won't play with them because of the color of their skin. Raising James and Heléna with a black identity will give them something of value no adversary could use against them or tear them down." Janel knew I was determined to make sure our children would not have their hopes, potential, or dreams taken from them or shattered in the event their black father was not nearby. I knew this experience firsthand. My parents did what they could to prepare my brother and I for it and protect us. It was important that we be prepared to do the same so James and Heléna would be protected. I could tell Janel understood my rationale. I remember her saying, "I never thought about that before. I just want to make sure they are not ashamed of me or my family." In retrospect, I can see why the prospect of children she brought into the world who could possibly deny her and her family's background would concern her and her family. Much to her credit, she realized that raising our son and daughter to identify black was in their best interest. Janel embraced and cultivated our son's and daughter's love of self. Our children grew up having the best of both worlds offered by our respective families. James' and Heléna's respective love for, and devotion to, their mother and her family remained strong. Our children are now adults. Their identities are strong. They understand who they are, where they come from, and the challenges they will encounter as a black man and black woman. Our posterity knows the struggle is real.

Chapter XII
I Have a Purpose

Dad and Mom never failed to remind my brother and I of our capabilities. My brother and I always knew we had distinct and unique purposes to fulfill in this world. Although our parents did their very best to shield us from much of the world's ugliness, it was not to be. Our adult lives have been filled with challenges and hardships. We were not immune from the "issues of life." Fortunately, we were heavily influenced by our parents' expectations. Throughout my childhood and early adult years, I wanted my life and my parents' lives to resemble something it wasn't. Our parents were hard-nosed, hard-working people who had no patience for nonsense and excuses. Neither were recipients of post-secondary degrees, although my father had some post-secondary experience. Nonetheless, it was commonplace for people to believe that my parents were *professional people*, and they were not. Oftentimes, people (e.g. teachers, neighbors, strangers, etc.) would draw some interesting conclusions about my parents, our household, and how my brother and I were raised, solely based on their interactions with us. Although I did not encourage these conclusions, I didn't go out of my way to correct them.

I remember my first year in college. It was 1983. I was sitting in the back row of the classroom. A philosophy professor, Dr. James Drane, asked me, "Murphy, you come from a wealthy family, don't you?" I was surprised by the blunt nature of his question in front of the entire class. I could feel the eyes of a predominantly white class directed on me. My response was deliberate and deflective. I recall saying, "I wouldn't say we are wealthy. My parents do okay." Upon reflecting, maybe he asked the question to elicit a response from which he could build the crux of his lecture. I wasn't sure. Then, I began to wonder what had I done or said to give this learned man the impression I was from a wealthy family? I was eighteen years old and trying to figure out who I was, like most people my age. I wasn't wearing expensive attire or jewelry. At the time, I didn't understand what made me stand out to this instructor in a class occupied by forty to forty-five other students. Was it because I was one of the few black students in the class? It's possible. As I recall, three out of forty-five students in the classroom were black. Was it because he took a genuine interest in my perspective? Maybe he did. I don't know. But it was at that moment that I began to realize people assumed a great deal about my upbringing that was not a reflection of my reality. People assumed my father was an attorney, partly because I aspired to be one. I didn't see the need to discourage or correct them. As I grew older, it only continued as my brother and I encountered and engaged people from various walks of life. Many of these conclusions, whether drawn by my peers, instructors, or employers, were based on the manner in which my brother and I were both able to effectively interact with people.

Many would attribute such ability to the rigors of formal education. The foundation of our respective abilities and knowledge is a product of the standards and expectations set by the parents who reared us.

Our parents are very different. Both have very different, albeit engaging, personalities—the kind that can effectively transcend politics and communities. I didn't grow up in a home where our sphere of human contact was limited to the black community. We did attend a predominantly black church, lived in black neighborhoods, and were always taught to remember and study black history, embrace black culture, and the black experience. Doing so was never at the expense of dismissing or devaluing the existence and experiences of others. Without us being aware of it, our parents provided us a very unusual and different upbringing that allowed my brother and myself to not only experience, understand, appreciate, and value others, but we were taught at a very young age not to allow anyone's opinion or viewpoints to determine our value or self-worth. We understood at an early age that we were not born in a box or being raised in one. Therefore, we didn't have to settle for living in one or acting like we did. To allow anyone who is unaware of our gifts to define our existence and future was reprehensible to our parents. We learned that every situation presented its own set of unique circumstances and people, and each required the most appropriate state of readiness.

As I reflected on Mom's life and her impact, I realized that she was and remains a true visionary. She was ahead of her time. She understood how she wanted to raise us. Her objective was to prepare her sons to be men. In short, she wanted us to be prepared for the world and know how to navigate it with strength and intelligence that would honor our family. Mom intentionally placed us in circumstances and situations we would not have always chosen for ourselves. She forced us out of our comfort zone at a very young age. Not even Dad could save us. She placed us in situations to meet and engage people who represented a wide demographic and possessed different perspectives and life experiences.

During our elementary and middle school years, we attended schools with children who were diagnosed with Down syndrome, cerebral palsy, and other physical limitations. This was an elementary and middle school in Buffalo, New York, located on the campus of Buffalo State University, where this population of special-needs students was integrated within our school's learning environment. My brother attended this school from the time he was in kindergarten. My parents didn't enroll me until I was in the fourth grade. Although most of this student population attended classes in separate classrooms, we often saw these students in the hallways, restrooms, the library, and the cafeteria. Like most of the other middle-school-age kids, I thought the behavior of these students was odd and even funny. I didn't always exhibit the proper sensitivity. I didn't have a true appreciation for this student population. Why? Because I didn't understand their condition. I didn't understand why their speech was difficult to understand. I recall mocking their gait and their inability to hold their head in a stable position. As I look back on my behavior and treatment of these students, I cannot help but think about how I and other students hurt their feelings. We didn't see them as people with emotions who suffered pain as a result of being mistreated. As a teenager, I later realized this population, in spite of their unique condition (e.g. the way they walked, communicated, and played), was no less valuable or important than anyone else. By the time I graduated from the eighth grade, I realized there was something unique about the world. It was broader and filled with people who were different from me, whose needs and concerns were more important than my own. I now realize my paradigm was being transformed.

This transformation continued when Mom desired to make our home a place of respite (e.g. long-term care) for adults with the same or similar conditions. I can't remember when it all began, or how and why my parents made this commitment to care for these strangers. I can vividly remember many of them. These "clients" would come live with us. Some would come for a few weeks. Some stayed for a year. Some stayed indefinitely. Some of the clients were permanent residents at a facility where their parents or caretakers placed them. Some were children of very famous people, and some were not. No matter, our parents made sure they were incorporated into our family like they were their children and our siblings. My mother referred to these clients as our "brothers" and "sisters." It seemed every new respite brought someone who was a different race and displayed a unique personality.

Mom was officially listed as the respite provider. This was a responsibility in which we all shared. Our new "brothers" and "sisters" were not just fed and provided shelter but they were all expected to live up to their capabilities, make their beds, brush their teeth, dress and feed themselves. With few exceptions, many of the clients displayed independence and were self-sufficient. We celebrated their birthdays, and they often remained with us through the holidays and traveled with our family. This experience, like so many others, was eye-opening and life-changing. It gave me a new and broader understanding of the value of human life. Their respective ethnicity and religious affiliations varied. Some were black. Some were white. They were male. They were female.

One client, whose care I was primarily responsible for during the summer of 1984, was an eight-year-old Japanese boy named Jean. Jean stayed with us the entire summer. I helped bathe and feed him. I took him everywhere with me, including dates. I had no choice. My girlfriend at the time appeared to prefer his company to mine.

Jean had this amazing personality. He had this mischievous grin and a smile a mile wide. He always laughed and was very affectionate. I don't remember him ever being upset. Whenever he wanted to know something or ask for something, Jean would tilt his head to the right, pronounce my name "Alridge," point to whatever he saw, whether it was an animal at the zoo or the ice cream truck he heard come down our street, and effectively communicate his desires. Mom would always say, "That boy got sense." She was right. It was the summer of Jean. I did not get paid for all the work. However, it did show me that I was capable of taking care of another human being.

We all witnessed and experienced the joy and laughter in every single client brought into our home. We received the unconditional love and affection from each person who entered and became an important part of our lives for a given season. It's not an overestimation to state that they forever changed our family unit for the better. I know it helped me understand the importance of being selfless and putting the needs of others before my own interests and desires.

Ultimately, these experiences helped me recognize and appreciate the unconditional love of my cousin, Pat, who has Down syndrome. When I was younger, my relationship with Pat was friendly, and we always embraced each other. Outside of an embrace and kiss on the cheek, that was it. Not anymore. My experiences have broadened my understanding and appreciation for my cousin. Now, it is Pat's effervescent joy and engaging smile and laughter that draws me to her every time I lay eyes on her. She has the gift to flip your world right-side up.

The experience of embracing differences is a lot easier said than done. Not until the security of your existence or comfort zone is shaken and disrupted are your beliefs and heart truly tested. But for being exposed to, and being entrusted with caring for, the life of a person who functions at a different physical and mental capacity, I'm not sure I would have learned that loving relationships can help us all successfully transform our attitudes and broaden our perspectives to understand and value the people you come into contact with throughout your life.

From childhood to early adulthood, we spent a great deal of time around the elders of our respective families. We were blessed to not only know our grandparents, great-grandparents, aunts, and uncles but developed and maintained very strong relationships with them. Between high school and college, two of my great uncles and my maternal grandfather moved into my parents' home and received full-time care. Some lived in our parents' home until the time of their passing. This multi-generational household became a regular occurrence. Caring for an older relative was challenging and posed inconveniences. It had to be frustrating at times for my parents. Nonetheless, they did it without expecting or receiving anything in return.

The first older relative I can remember my parents providing a respite or care for was my Uncle Henry Fondren. I remember my Uncle Henry fondly. Uncle Henry was stubborn and deemed crazy by my other relatives. He was the relative that, when his name was mentioned, people who knew him would shake their head, displaying disbelief and grin. Nothing else needed to be said. I remember him as eccentric. Others might even describe him as bombastic. His personality never got in the way of his love for my brother and me. He cared for us and enjoyed spending time with us. For a period of time, he moved in with our family and looked after us while our parents worked. I remember being in the sixth grade. I didn't know why he was living with us. It didn't matter to me and Terrance. He played with us. He taught us how to play pool, checkers, and make biscuits with syrup. He was the strongest old man I ever met. I remember, no matter how often I tried, I could not beat him in arm wrestling. When I got older and returned home from school, I would take it upon myself to visit Uncle Henry. Doing so was not without its risks. It was downright dangerous. Whether it was because of his age or paranoia, Uncle Henry would sleep on a couch in his living room. The doorway entering his upstairs apartment was located directly across from the couch where he slept. Additionally, Uncle Henry would set up a spring gun contraption that would discharge toward the doorway in the event someone would try to break in. Additionally, he slept with a revolver under his pillow. Thus, it was a wise move to make sure Uncle Henry knew you were coming to visit or to announce yourself clearly if you were standing on the opposite side of his doorway. Uncle Henry was an adventurer, much to the dismay of people who would try to get him to slow down. To the best of my knowledge, he never allowed his age or a physical ailment to get the best of him or determine how he would live his life. Uncle Henry taught me to embrace life and everything it has to offer, and never allow anyone to stop you. He was truly resilience in action.

While I was still in college, my Great-Uncle Percy moved in with my parents. Every other weekend, I had a standing appointment to return to Buffalo, visit with Uncle Percy, and give him a haircut and shave. Even at his advanced age, he always knew when I was coming to town. My time spent with him illustrated not only the reciprocity in our relationship but also demonstrated how two individuals—eighty and twenty-one years of age respectively—can develop a rapport and a mutual respect for one another. In return, Uncle Percy would never fail to take the opportunity to give me his unsolicited advice about politics and women. Although I didn't have the privilege of knowing Uncle Percy as long as I did Uncle Henry, the impact on my life was no less significant.

Even today, people comment on the ease with which my brother and I engage senior citizens. Simply, it's a respect thing. I remember an occasion when I was about fourteen years old, when we were going to visit an elderly member of my mother's family. I recall not being too happy about it. I wanted to do something else. It was at that moment that my mother told me something that would forever alter my paradigm about how I viewed seniors. She said, "It may not seem like it now, but you will get older someday. Think about how you will want to be treated when you get older." From that day forward, my attitude changed. I recall that, no matter whom we would visit and why, my value and appreciation for what senior citizens could show and teach me grew. That conversation inspired a change in my attitude and perspective. When I would return from college on weekends, etc., my father would be the first to ask me if I had visited my grandmothers (his mother and grandmother) while I was home. Thus, I would make those visits my highest priority whenever I returned. Oftentimes, I would stop by to see my grandparents before I came home to see my parents.

An experience that gave me a greater appreciation for the lives of older adults was a *Psychology of Aging* course I took as an undergraduate. One of the course requirements was to interview a senior member of our family. I chose to interview my Great-Grandmother Emma Harris, aka "Momma." It was the 1984 fall semester, and I was nineteen years old. Earlier that spring, her husband, my Great-Grandfather

Andrew, "Pop" Harris, passed away. I didn't know it at the time, but this assignment would be an informative one for me, and a timely and cathartic one for Momma. It wasn't until I interviewed her that I had any knowledge of the nature of her upbringing, other than what I would casually overhear when it was discussed among her children (grandparents, aunts, uncles and cousins).

Following Pop's passing in the spring of 1984, people began to notice how much more communicative Momma became. She began to exert considerably more influence over her household and express her likes and dislikes. What I didn't know was that Momma's life and marriage with Pop did not provide her with the emotional and spiritual fulfillment one would think would exist between people who had been married for over fifty years. My great-grandparents lived on the east side of Buffalo, New York. They owned a two-story home they occupied with their son, my Uncle Billy. Their home was large. I remember the back of the house being filled with fishing and hunting equipment. Pop would maintain a large garden in the back-yard. When I would visit, my great-grandfather and "his" company would occupy the front room. Rarely did Momma enter this area of the house. She would sit in the adjoining room, receive visitors there, and would offer pieces of candy and snacks to me and my cousins. I don't want to give the impression that she never ventured into the front room. She did. During my family's weekly Saturday visits, it was rare to see her enter that area of the house. She remained in the adjoining room and would look forward to watching *Hee Haw* every Saturday evening. It was her favorite television show. Before living and raising their family in Buffalo, New York, my great-grandparents lived in Camden, South Carolina, where they were sharecroppers. Sharecroppers rented small plots of land from landowners in return for a portion of their crops. Great-grandma was Cherokee Indian. Her skin color and beautiful long hair reflected her Native American features. She was petite and always presented a warm smile and a gentle disposition.

Pop was of mixed racial heritage. He was black, albeit very light-skinned. According to my family, he was also part Jewish. On more than one occasion, I remember the older members of our family discussing how often my great-grandfather passed for white while living in South Carolina, before an "incident" forced him and his family to migrate north to Buffalo. Pop was an avid outdoorsman and farmer. He was equipped with skills and expertise to live off the land to take care of his family. The vegetable gardens he and Momma grew in the backyard of their home were legendary. Depending upon the person you asked, Pop was described as ornery and mean. However, there was never a doubt about how much he loved his family.

What I thought I knew about my great-grandparents' personal history and relationship with one another paled in comparison to what I was about to discover. As I asked Momma a series of questions about her life, it occurred to me that, but for this assignment, I'm not sure I would have ever had this conversation with her. She shared details about her life growing up, meeting Pop, getting married, having and raising her children, and also the loneliness she experienced during the early stages of her marriage. She said, "I did not have a lot of friends." Upon reflection, if I had been more mature and intuitive, I would have asked her a follow-up question, "Why didn't you have a lot of friends?" I did not. As she discussed her experiences, I couldn't help but notice how much she became inquisitive about why I was taking so much interest in her life. She was almost amazed and bewildered at the thought of someone wanting to know about her life and thoughts. As I reflect back on it now, Momma was being provided a voice. She was being empowered to define her own existence and value. The few hours we spent conversing and exploring one another's interests had a transformational impact on us both. She had a story to share with me that left an indelible mark on my life. I was gaining the benefit of her wisdom, as she shared the pain and joys of her life. In return, Momma was empowered with a long-awaited opportunity to share the story of her existence and life experiences with her great-grandson, on her own terms, and in her voice. She was not relying upon the knowledge and respectful words of her family. Before my very eyes, I had the privilege of seeing and hearing an eighty-year-old woman defining her life.

Momma laughed more than I can ever remember. Over the few hours we spent together, she spoke with a level of conviction, while exhibiting the freedom and strength I never witnessed before. I often wonder did it have something to do with Pop passing? Did she share herself with me because I expressed an interest to know something about her life? At the time, it was an assignment for a grade. It was an interview I was required to complete during a weekend visit home from school. Never did I think it would change the nature of my relationship with her and the course of my life.

As a result, subsequent visits with Momma became more than just a hug and a kiss on the cheek. I no longer sat idle with her while she watched her favorite television show, interrupted by a few casual questions I felt forced to ask. Our relationship flourished. I was able to talk to her about my friends and girlfriends. I welcomed the opportunity to introduce her to my fiancée, who would later become my wife. In fact, she became more inquisitive about me and my interests. My relationship with her became one of the most valued in my life at a time when her simple words and laughter helped me to successfully navigate challenging circumstances. Momma didn't have the privilege of attending college. She didn't have a formal high school education. She was married by the time she was sixteen years old. She was a very strong, wise, and intelligent woman who also experienced loneliness at times that I can now comprehend and appreciate. She took great joy in her children, grandchildren, great-grandchildren, and great-great grandchildren. No matter what any member of the family may have done, she exemplified forgiveness and love with ease, and she did so unconditionally.

My maternal grandfather is Elvage M. Fondren, Sr. To those who know him throughout the southeastern part of the United States, he is known as Bishop. With the exception of a few family trips to Memphis, Tennessee and Mississippi during my adolescent years, I didn't have the privilege of spending as much time around him. After I graduated from college, the frequency of my trips to see him increased. He was an evangelist, shepherding multiple churches, which frequently kept him on the road seven days a week. The moments I spent with him were always memorable. Being with him, especially traveling throughout the city of Memphis, was always a journey through "black history." He took me to landmarks I would never forget, like the Lorraine Motel, where Dr. Martin Luther King was assassinated. He also showed me the location where black sanitation workers, who took refuge in the back of a sanitation truck to get out of the rain, were crushed to death when the compactor mechanism of the truck was triggered. According to Grandaddy, black sanitation workers were compelled to take refuge in the rear of garbage trucks during inclement weather. The city of Memphis once barred black sanitation workers from using shelter stops in residential neighborhoods. His recollections of both tragedies were descriptive and horrific. Hearing about these injustices and others like them would become a constant reminder of how important it is to not only value one's life but to be willing to lay it down to honor the sacrifices of others who came before you. He taught me that honoring the sacrifices of others is not limited by one's race, age, or education. My grandfather's teachings proved to be prophetic.

On January 18, 1994, the retrial of Byron D La Beckwith, the man charged with the murder of Medgar Evers, was set to begin. At the time, Grandaddy resided in Batesville, Panola County, Mississippi. Granddaddy was one of over 500 similarly situated residents who received a summons to report for jury duty. The case would be prosecuted in Hinds County, Mississippi. The atmosphere surrounding the retrial was described as hostile and intimidating. People viewed the retrial as an opportunity to secure justice. Others viewed the retrial as a nuisance and unfair to a man of senior age like De La Beckwith. Granddaddy joined his fellow Panolians at the Panola County Courthouse for *voire dire*. *Voire Dire* literally means to *speak the truth*, and describes the jury selection process. On January 26, 1994, the jury was picked, and Granddaddy was one of them. He and his fellow jurors were transported to Hinds County and sequestered throughout the duration of the trial. For approximately a week and a half, he and the other jurors were cut off from their families and media. Granddaddy would be selected to serve as the foreperson of the jury. At the conclusion of the trial and following deliberations, the jury returned a verdict of guilty on February 5, 1994. At the time of his service on this jury, Granddaddy was seventy years old. He didn't seek to be a juror or campaign for the role of foreperson. Simply, he was prepared to serve when called. None of us know the time we will be called or appointed to fulfill the task of service. Many of his fellow Panolians sought to avoid and get out of this obligation for a wide variety of reasons. Grandaddy did not. He simply chose to make himself available to serve. He became a part of history and ensured that, although justice may be delayed, it is never denied.

In order for me to appreciate and value the "older folks" in my life, I had to distance myself from my "I know that. . ." attitude and recognize the relevance of their experiences, and that their ways of thinking were not obsolete and remain relevant to navigating today's world. The dynamics of these intergenerational relationships not only continue to guide and direct my decisions but I attribute my personal and professional development and success to them. Although advanced age should garner respect, it is not the sole criterion that determines a person's value. It is the wisdom they all possessed that resulted from the knowledge accumulated throughout their lifetimes. Thank you, family!

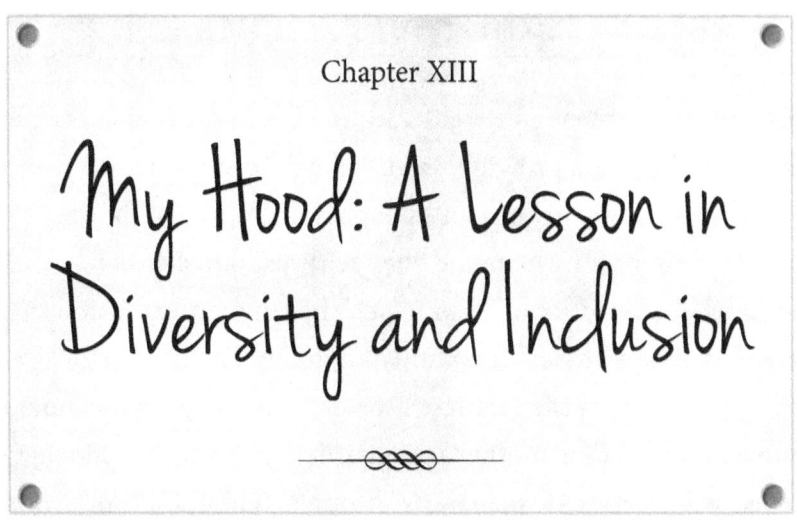

Chapter XIII
My Hood: A Lesson in Diversity and Inclusion

Like anything else worth pursuing, working toward a diverse and inclusive society is a responsibility and journey we all share. And I'm not convinced it is something you can persuade people to accept legislatively or mandate with a court order. It's a matter of the heart. An understanding of these issues requires maturity, risk, and a willingness to engage people. Diversity and inclusiveness are critical to helping us understand who we are and who we are capable of becoming. Diversity and inclusion do not require an agreement on every political or social issue. All it requires is an understanding and acceptance that people and their experiences and viewpoints, no matter how ridiculous or objectionable to our sensibilities, have value. Our mother and father made our introduction to diversity and inclusion. Before they became the favorite buzzwords at universities and in the workplace, these concepts were our living reality without us knowing it.

Throughout our childhood, we became intimately familiar with other kids and families who were Jewish, Italian, German, Irish, and Polish, etc. You name it, we were immersed or exposed to a variety of different people and traditions. We spent our formative and adolescent years growing up in a neighborhood that reflected a wide array of ethnic groups and people from all walks of life. As we became familiar with them and they with us, our neighbors, people outside of our traditional "family set," became an extension of our household. The phrase "like family" is often overused. However, it accurately describes the relationships between our family and a few of our neighbors. Our mother was guarded. But she shared what she believed was pertinent to share with our neighbors. Mom's willingness to be "neighborly" came with considerable risks. It was 1978. The neighborhood was predominantly white, and the likelihood of a black family encountering rejection and hostility among our new neighbors was likely. In some instances, she initiated contact with our new neighbors. Not only was she receptive to establishing new relationships, she went a step further. She was open to learning about, and making, connections with people next door and across the street. Again, this is a woman who did not submit to fear. Her initiative or receptiveness to a neighbor's invitation was an investment from which my brother and our children are continuing to reap benefits. The lessons we were learning at home were being reinforced as we came into contact with our neighbors.

For example, our neighbors always knew what week and day we were receiving our report cards. I would wonder (not out loud of course), "How in the hell did Ms. So and So know when I was getting my report card?" Instantly, I knew. "Ma must have said something." Our white neighbors wanted to know our grades, and there was no denying them this information. If they didn't get this information from us directly, Ma would be sure to inform them. Interestingly, I can't imagine a time when our neighbors were not genuinely concerned about our welfare. They were invested in us getting a good education and not falling prey to the temptations and misdeeds of some of their own children and grandchildren. We were covered. There was nothing we could do, or get away with, that our neighbors could not or did not find out about.

Within close proximity of my parents' home lived the Puiuses (Romanian-Jews), Bergmans (German-Jews), Penningtons (African-American), Ms. Cirrincione (Italian), the Braatzes (German) and the Murrays (Irish), and a host of others up and down our street. A few of these families immigrated to the United States from their respective "old country" or at a minimum were one generation removed from being immigrants to the United States. At twelve or thirteen years old, their races and ethnicities were not a relevant factor to me. I never gave it much thought until my early adult years. They were gracious and, most importantly, respectful of our family, and we were required to reciprocate the courtesies. The relationships with each household did not form immediately. It took time. I have to believe there was a respective feeling-out process. They checked us out, and I am certain my parents (Ma) checked them out. From 1978 through 1994, the relationships with each family grew at its own pace. All of it was spearheaded by our mother's boldness, enthusiasm, and kindness. She saw how mutually beneficial it was to get to know people, and she was just getting started.

As our family's interaction with our neighbors increased, the relationships changed. As I was approaching my early adult years, I vividly remember our mother excitedly extending invitations to each and every one of our neighbors to attend holiday festivities, high school and college graduation parties, our wedding reception, and their twenty-fifth wedding anniversary celebration. Invitations were accepted and our parents were honored by their attendance and gifts. Having black and white folks in the same house, backyard, or banquet hall, and enjoying each other's company was not an isolated or unusual dynamic in our family's life. In return, our parents made sure our family reciprocated. We intentionally recognized and honored our neighbors' cultural and religious traditions (e.g. Chanukah), birthdays, and weddings. There were times when I would occasionally hear my black friends and cousins say, "They trying to be white." or "Why do y'all have so many white friends?" It never occurred to me that these relationships or connections made us less black or "not down for the cause." Every opportunity for engagement provided my brother and me with a different view of the world that existed outside the black community. Unbeknownst to me, I was being provided a look—access to different traditions and history of people who didn't look like me or whose ancestry I didn't share. Our neighbors, for an assortment of their own reasons, opened their lives and shared their personal histories and experiences that offered a different type of inspiration.

The Puius family lived next door. They moved in shortly after we did in the early 1980s. Mr. and Mrs. Puius's immigrated to the United States from Romania. It was my first time meeting anyone from Eastern Europe, let alone Romania. The only relevance Romania had for me at the time was that I knew it was the country that produced Olympic gold medal gymnast, Nadia Comaneci. Meeting this family expanded my world. The Puius family left an indelible impression on me. Mr. Puius was an engineer. He spoke with a very heavy accent. His wife and my mother became very good friends, as did my brother, Terrance, and their son. Mr. Puius was the first to celebrate our academic achievements and cajoled us at every turn to take advantage of every opportunity we were provided. We had always been encouraged at home, at church, and within our family. But this was the first time I remember someone outside of school and my usual cultural environment challenging me academically and intellectually. He was the consummate cheerleader. Mrs. Puius was a stay-at-home mother. I recall Mr. Puius being an older gentleman. His wife was about fifteen years his junior. They were different from any other married couples I had encountered, even my parents. Mr. Puius doted on Mrs. Puius. He worshipped her in a positive and healthy way. They were never shy about showing a healthy respect and affection for one another. My impressions were affirmed one day when I heard my mother say, "Jewish men love their wives." I didn't understand the context of that statement then, but I think I do now. Mom's knowledge of, and familiarity with, the Jewish culture provided her insight into the dynamic of a marriage relationship that is built on promoting the spiritual and physical health of a woman. Was this a moment of transformation? Is this something from which we can all learn and apply to our marriages and day-to-day lives? I'd like to believe that most reasonable people would agree and resoundingly say, "Yes!" Little did I know that observing aspects of the Puius's marriage began a transformation and provided me a healthy framework about how to think about marriage conceptually and practically.

The Murray family lived one house down from us next to the Puius family. Although our contact with the Murrays was intermittent, it was very respectful. I remember seeing Mr. Murray dressed in a suit and tie every day and driving off to work. Although I didn't know what he did for a living, I assumed he worked in an office. Most of their children were older and in college, except for their youngest daughter, who was about my brother's age at the time we moved in.

I recall Mrs. Murray being a very nice, hospitable lady. Although I didn't know much about her, I always saw her as the quintessential stay-at-home mother whose highest priority was raising their children. They projected a very traditional lifestyle. Albeit quiet and unassuming, they were helpful and generous.

Mr. and Mrs. Braatz lived across the street. Their home was situated on the corner, diagonally from our home. The Braatzes owned a bakery in North Buffalo. Mr. Braatz was known as "Smiley" to everyone. His nickname fit perfectly. Every time I would see him, he always had a smile on his face. When we would call him Mr. Braatz, he wouldn't have it. He wanted to be called Smiley. But our mother wouldn't have that. She never permitted us to call an adult by their first name or a nickname. Once, when my mother was not around, he told me I could call him Smiley. His personality matched his nickname. Smiley was very considerate and cool for an old guy. He had this mischievous, child-like character to him. He and my brother hit it off, also. If I had to guess, Smiley had to be a ladies' man back in the day. He reminded me of the cool uncle in every family who maintains a childlike and playful disposition that kids and young people find appealing. The Braatzes also had what appeared to be the biggest house in the neighborhood. It was white with yellow trim. The appearance of it matched Mr. and Mrs. Braatz's charm and personalities. At the time we moved into the neighborhood, most of their children were grown and were no longer living at home. As my mother and Mrs. Braatz grew closer, and with good ole Smiley being an effervescent mainstay in our lives, life was not boring on Covington Road.

Mr. and Mrs. Bergman lived in a beautiful home, one house down, and across the street from us. While I was in high school, Mr. and

Mrs. Bergman hired me to cut their lawn. One of the many things I remember about the Bergmans is that they were both very proper and exuded class. Mr. Bergman was very polite and reserved. And Mrs. Bergman was also very nice and polite. Unlike Mr. Bergman, she was not what I would call reserved. She was a great deal more animated than her husband. She was a character and had what I would call "swag." She not only enjoyed life—she attacked it. No matter when, and under what circumstances, she was always impeccably and tastefully dressed. What distinguished Mrs. Bergman from others was her fearless nature. She never had to say, "I am a strong woman." You just knew it. In particular, she enjoyed talking about, and sharing, her experiences growing up as a little girl in Germany. As I was stopping over one afternoon to pick up my payment for cutting their grass, Mrs. Bergman was sharing aspects of her childhood with me about being in a concentration camp. She asked me if I knew anything about concentration camps. I told her I had heard of them. She asked if I had ever met someone who had been in one? I told her, "No." At that moment, she slowly rolled up the sleeve of her blouse and showed me what looked like a combination of numbers or letters on her arm. It was one of the most remarkable and memorable experiences of my life to meet and know someone who spent time in a Nazi concentration camp as a little girl. For the first time in the ten years of living on this block, I saw a side of Mrs. Bergman I had never witnessed before. Initially, I thought I was witnessing sadness. Maybe I was. I wasn't sure. What this moment with a sixty-plus-year-old woman taught me was not to be afraid to be vulnerable and transparent about your life and experiences, no matter how painful. Simply, our pain can be someone else's gain. Mrs. Bergman let her guard down and shared a vulnerable side of herself with a sixteen-year-old black boy. Why? I am sure she had her reasons. Little did she know that this interaction put a face on a holocaust some are still trying to sanitize and make palatable. But for my relationships with people like the Bergmans and the Puiuses. I'm not sure I would appreciate the historical significance of the Holocaust.

The Penningtons lived directly across the street from our family. Both worked for the city of Buffalo in different capacities. Mr. Pennington worked for the city as an accountant, and Mrs. Pennington was a schoolteacher. Not long after we moved into the neighborhood, I remember she and her husband were the first to greet and welcome us with a housewarming present. Mr. Pennington reminded me of one of the older men (e.g. ushers, deacons, etc.) at the church we attended. He was thin, tall, almost stoic, and a bit intimidating. He had this anal, type-A characteristic about himself. Everything about him reflected a need for precision and perfection. His home, car, yard, or physical appearance was never out of order. At the time, I never gave it a second thought how the appearance of order in his life would have an influence on me. But it did. When he worked in his yard, his appearance was neat and orderly. He never looked disheveled or out of place. Additionally, he had the personality to match. Unlike Mrs. Pennington, it was challenging to connect with him socially. He was awkward. What finally allowed me to develop a level of comfort and rapport with Mr. Pennington was when I would delve into his passions for thoroughbred racing, baseball, and golf. Raising these subjects with him would flip a switch, and he would turn on the personality and charm that was rarely seen. We grew up playing little league, and our father's favorite sport is baseball. It was a means by which my father, my brother, and me could connect with him. What I found most intriguing about Mr. Pennington was his passion for thoroughbred racing and golf. Mr. Pennington attended the Kentucky Derby annually. I quickly became familiar with phrases like "the run for the roses" and the "triple crown." When I was in the seventh grade, golf was not on my radar. Outside of the experience of seeing a few black professionals play in tournaments on television, and at an old local, municipal course, I didn't know much about it. Until Mr. Pennington, I didn't know anyone who played it. It was the first time I actually knew a black person who played the game. He installed a putting green in his yard. I had never seen or heard of anyone, especially black people, doing such a thing. It was odd to me at the time. He not only played but encouraged and offered to teach me, my brother, and father to play. More often than not, we repeatedly declined his invitations, rather than accept them. I ask myself all the time why didn't I accept Mr. Pennington's offers? I now realize that I allowed the shortsightedness associated with someone else's perception about golf kill my interest in it before I gave it an opportunity to take root.

Mrs. Pennington took an instant liking to my mother, and my mother to her. Out of all our neighbors, I always believed my mother had the closest relationship with her. She became like a sister to Mom. Although I was not always privy to their conversations or how they spent time together, Mom had a tremendous amount of respect for Mrs. Pennington. I would always refer to her as Mrs. "P." Mrs. P was very proper and dignified. She had an aura about her, and she commanded everyone's attention and respect. When she spoke, you didn't. You listened attentively. You didn't have a choice. She made sure of it. Mrs. P was old school. She didn't tolerate excuses from her students or from us. She expected the very best from all young people. She had every right to do so. Mrs. P attended, and graduated from, Clark University in Atlanta, Georgia. I remember how proud she was to tell everyone she was a product of Clark. Although Mrs. Pennington could be soft-spoken, she had a way of making sure you knew she was in charge. She would call you into correction quickly if the circumstances required it.

I always viewed Mrs. Pennington as a mentor to Mom. Up until the time she passed away, they remained very close. You would have thought my mother and her were raised in the same household. They both abhorred everything and anything that would reflect negatively on the black community. It was in Mrs. Pennington that our mother found her equal. She was someone who would cultivate the vision our mother had for us. Mrs. Pennington inspired our mother and provided her insight and wisdom at critical moments when our mother needed it most.

In time, Mr. and Mrs. Pennington became like another set of parents to me and Terrance. They both looked out for us, always inquired about the status of our academic performances, behavior, etc., attended our high school and college graduations, and celebrated milestones in our lives. We reciprocated their love and concern by caring for them both as the need arose. There was no doubt that the Penningtons brought revelation to our lives and shaped our thinking. They were a breath of fresh air that forever opened our family's hearts and minds.

Finally, there was Mrs. Cirrincione. Sometimes, we referred to her as "Ms. Eva." She was an old school, petite Italian woman whose passion for life was as evident as her exuberant and boisterous personality. When she opened her mouth, everyone in the neighborhood could hear her. She lived next door. Ms. Eva was not married. Her children were older, and she lived alone. Some might have described her as bossy. I never thought of her that way. Ms. Eva embraced life. I remember her laughing all the time and being in a festive mood. She was always going places and enjoying life. That was her way. What I do remember is that Ms. Eva never tired. She never stayed at home. She was always on the go. Grass didn't grow under her feet, primarily because I was hired to cut it for her. In keeping with her unique style and genuine personality, she embraced and welcomed us into her life. As we became a part of her life, she became a part of ours. I'm not sure we ever had a choice in the matter. Ms. Eva, like a lot of the older women with whom my parents developed relationships, earned the title of "Mom."

No matter the variations in ethnicity, religious, or cultural backgrounds, I could see there was a shared expectation, a standard, that all of our neighbors maintained for themselves and our neighborhood. These expectations were the product of the collective character that was cultivated and maintained by the people who lived in this North Buffalo neighborhood. There was no homeowner's association enforcing regulations and imposing punitive measures to make sure everyone stayed in compliance with a list of rules and policies. I don't recall anyone ever admonishing and reminding my parents to mow and edge our lawn or demanding that we maintain our property in a particular condition. Our parents had high expectations and standards for themselves. They were not derived from the demands of our neighbors. Nor were our parents trying to adopt a mentality for the purpose of fitting in at the expense of forsaking their own identities. Our parents' expectations and standards were self-imposed and founded in their own hopes and vision for themselves and our family. It just so happened our parents' expectations and standards were substantially similar to those who lived in this neighborhood.

It would be ridiculous to assert that a physical blending and co-existence of different people into a neighborhood requires an agreement on every issue or aspect of life. All that is required for people to live together is a common understanding and a commitment to be reasonable and exercise, dare I say, "courtesy." Mom was very adamant about respecting the property and homes of our neighbors. Where we lived previously, it was not unheard of for kids to play football and other games in the middle of the street. Once we moved into this North Buffalo neighborhood, Mom didn't want us to bring that same mentality with us. Although our neighbors didn't appear to mind, our parents quickly helped us to understand and see how people took care of their property. From Mom's perspective, an infringement upon one person's household (e.g. walking on, and across, their lawn, kicking a football and hitting the side of their home, etc.) was an infringement upon every household, including our own.

We were immersed within a diverse community that shared common expectations and standards and, more importantly, a common vision. How does a common vision transcend different households occupied by different people with different political and cultural paradigms? It may be impossible to identify one factor that aptly explains how and why we had so much in common with our neighbors. It was a willingness of people to make a commitment to engage their neighbors and cultivate relationships.

We witnessed how our parents cultivated and maintained relationships with people who were of different races, religions, and political ideology, and they did it effectively without submitting to the temptation of pretending to be someone they were not. I could tell that those around us held our parents in high regard. They were heavily invested in how they carried themselves and maintained our home. They were always complimented on the condition of the inside and outside of their home. I often reflect on these times and wonder if our neighbors were making this statement because they were surprised a black family took such responsibility in the care of their home, or if they were relieved that our presence would not be detrimental to their property values. Maybe it was a little bit of both and . . . maybe they were being truly sincere. Dad and Mom were adept at illustrating how the dynamics of human interaction provides the opportunity to realize the potential we possess and the vision we can establish for ourselves.

The vision of this North Buffalo neighborhood was a product of the commitment to human interaction. We saw it begin with the willingness of our parents and our neighbors to engage one another and remain open to transforming their thoughts, beliefs, perceptions, and experiences to say, "Hello, my name is. . ." This simple act set in to motion a chain of events that allowed us to rise above life's challenges. It didn't require forsaking the values, beliefs, or experiences that made us different, or to be a "sell out." Our parents, as well as their words, are a constant reminder of what they endured and from whom we descended. Maintaining our respect and dignity was of paramount importance; however, it was not to be at the expense of tearing down another person or family, in order to help propel us forward.

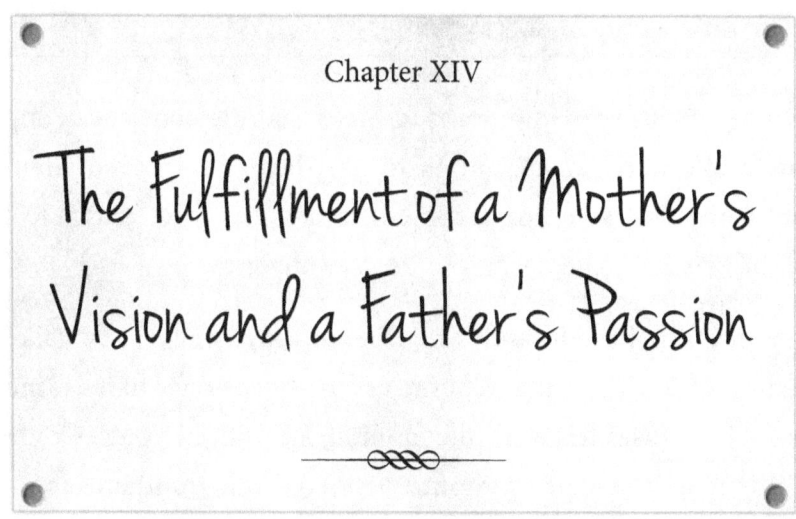

Chapter XIV

The Fulfillment of a Mother's Vision and a Father's Passion

Early childhood experts agree that early childhood experiences have lasting emotional and psychological effects. Early childhood experiences are often referred to as positive and negative. Either way, parents are in the best possible position to "set the table" for children during their formative years.

Throughout our childhood, Terrance and I were required to read a lot. I don't recall enjoying reading as a kid. My mother would suggest otherwise. Like most kids during the 1970s and 80s, I preferred to watch television, especially with the onset of cable television. In college, it became clear that the content on television and movies could not be relied upon to accurately depict the realities of the world. Through reading, I noticed how my knowledge of vocabulary and spelling exceeded the abilities of my peers. White strangers who would hear my brother or me speak would go out of their way and comment to my mother and father about the sophistication of our speech and the quality with which we articulated our words. The "compliments" would entail, "He speaks well; he is so articulate" or "I was surprised at how well he speaks." Remarkably, the "compliments" continue. It was very important to Mom that her sons speak appropriately. We were not permitted to use slang. She was so adamant about it that we were not permitted to use the word "ain't." To this day, she bristles if she hears it uttered by anyone.

Mom never believed—and still doesn't—in using "baby talk" to communicate with children. Some psychologists refer to it as "motherese." She refuses to use it to communicate with her pets. Contrary to some language experts, Mom considered this [motherese] . . . to be condescending or unrealistic in comparison to adult speech . . .[1] Mom would lose her mind listening to adults speak to children in a cartoon oriented, high-pitched voice to coax or cajole their children to do something or discover what they wanted. Even today, I watch how she communicates with children, and she remains adamant that adults should always communicate with children, regardless of age, by using correct grammar.

As a teenager, the use of slang was not a big deal and an everyday occurrence when we were hanging out with friends. God help us if she ever heard either of us utter the word "n____r" or any variation of it. If we did, she would come down on us hard. From her perspective and experience, the use of oppressive language had no place in the mind and on the tongue of an articulate, intelligent black man. Speaking appropriately everywhere (e.g. school, church, the street, etc.) was expected and required. No matter how often I heard, "You talk like you are white," we knew that speaking in any other form (at least in her presence) would result in receiving a loving reminder upside the head. She helped us to understand that we are all measured

---

1. Catherine E. Laing, The Conversation, http://www.cnn.com/2016/12/06/health/why-baby-talk-is-good/

by the knowledge and use of our words. The way we communicate opens doors, provides opportunities and access to environments that would otherwise be inaccessible.

A diverse environment is filled with people of different races and cultural influences. It requires a level of understanding and appreciation of unique perspectives and preferences. This level of understanding can only be achieved by having a command of the English language. A command of language can transform a person's mind and attitude and subsequently lead to the acquisition of understanding and wisdom.

Our parents never allowed a lack of resources or where we lived to dictate or determine whether we would have access to different experiences or people. Prior to 9/11, our accessibility to parts of Canada from the city of Buffalo was unfettered. Throughout my childhood and into my early twenties, trips to Ontario were commonplace. The province of Ontario became a second home. It was where we experienced a general appreciation for the great outdoors. Spending time outdoors became as natural to our family as breathing is for our survival. It was something we grew up doing and enjoying as a family. We were often joined on these camping trips by our aunts, uncles, and cousins. It was a tradition unlike any other. Every family owned a StarCraft camper, tents, Coleman stoves and lanterns, sleeping bags, boats, etc. Imagine over a half dozen African American families, composed of a minimum of four per family, arriving at a campsite in Canada. Today, my cousins and I jokingly refer to it as the invasion that changed Canada. From the time we were old enough to walk, we camped, fished, hiked, and some of the family hunted. Outside of the recreational benefits, our time spent in Canada provided us the opportunity to see how the cultures of the American and Canadian people were similar and distinguishable from one another. Most importantly, we learned the importance and value of cultivating and maintaining life-long relationships with the Canadians we met.

Like our American neighbors in Buffalo, our Canadian friends became an extension of our family. One couple I vividly remember was Edith and Charlie Teeple, an older couple who enjoyed life and people. I remember Edith having such an infectious personality. Although she was short in stature, she was larger than life. Her husband, Charlie, was tall, friendly, and thoughtful. They both enjoyed camping, each other's companionship, their dog, as well as the time spent with our families. This relationship yielded dividends beyond our family's expectations. From the beginning of our relationship with the Teeples, my brother and I referred to them as Mr. and Mrs. Teeple. Although they encouraged my brother and I to call them by their first names, Charlie and Edith, our parents, Mom in particular, would not allow it. As our family's relationship grew with the Teeples, we were privileged to call them "Grandma Teeple" and "Grandpa Teeple." My brother and I already had grandparents and great-grandparents. But the Teeples were no less significant in our lives. For whatever reason, they loved us like family. I remember they both traveled to Buffalo and showed up at my graduation party and other family milestones. The kindness and love exhibited by the Teeples and other Canadians helped broadened my understanding of a world beyond the United States. I don't recall subjects like politics, race, socio-economic status, or occupation being sources of division. Maybe they were; I don't know. I was probably too immature to recognize it if it did arise anyway. We were too busy having a good time. The moments I spent in Canada were critical to understanding and experiencing relationships with people who did not share my skin color or societal experiences. Although I never asked my parents how and why they thought so fondly of people from this other country, it occurred to me that these family trips were a part of a greater plan.

In 2017, I was speaking with my cousin. She shared some insight with me about Mom I had never considered until authoring this book. She said, "All mothers have hopes and dreams for their children." Then, my cousin said, "But your mother had a vision for you and Terrance." My cousin was correct. Mom gave Terrance and me all she had to give and more. Her investment went beyond the basic necessities of providing a hot meal and getting us off to school. Her vision prepared us to understand the world in which we lived and equipped us to overcome challenges we would encounter. Our mother was more than a dreamer; she was a visionary who had a mission to raise two boys into men who would mature and shake free of the limitations that others tried to impose. She faithfully sowed the right seed at the right time and under the right conditions from the moment of our births. Her timing was impeccable. A lot of people, including us, could not appreciate or understand the mystery of our mother's mind at times. Sometimes, I don't think she always understood it or could clearly articulate it, but she knew the end game. Whatever she sowed (e.g. time, energy, money, etc.), she made sure it was not in vain. She was our "sower." She set standards and had expectations for the two of us, and we were required to adhere to them. If not, we would incur a wrath I would not wish on my enemy. As my brother, Terrance, points out, no matter where we were, and/or the company we kept, we knew where the line was, and how close we came to approaching it. We straddled it. But we knew that, if we crossed it and did not conform our conduct to Mom's standards and expectations, there would be hell to pay. If she was the sower, we were the soil. She made sure that seed remained rooted. If we were "hard-headed" and tried to do things our way, we were inclined to bring a great deal of trouble on our heads.

Mom had a high school diploma. And although she didn't attend college, she was intelligent, insightful, and, most importantly, determined. She had every intention of making sure my brother and I had the opportunities she did not. She effectively cultivated her hopes and expectations for us by engaging a network of people she encountered every day. Unbeknownst to us, our mother was the quintessential networker before networking was a "thing." Her innate gift is cultivating relationships with people. People were drawn to my mother's passion and energy. She is truly a worker. She seized opportunities that allowed her to avail herself to people and the resources they possessed. I recall how often she attended meetings, listened attentively, and asked questions to the point of being a nuisance. She was determined to understand how "things" worked, who people were, and what they knew.

She was adamant about my brother and me not being afraid to make inquiries and ask questions. I was somewhat shy when I was younger. Mom forced us to try new things, go to new places, and embrace new experiences. My propensity for shyness dissipated. She frowned upon being "stagnant" or "settling." She expected us to demonstrate maturity and act with intellectual sophistication. Although she enjoyed the simple things in life, she didn't want to do the simple things every day or week, or go to the same places. She helped us to understand that embracing new and unfamiliar situations is the essence of life. Every day brings new challenges and people into our lives. We have to be prepared for such encounters when they arise. Once I understood and accepted the reality of her expectations, I realized that it wasn't shyness that was hindering me; it was fear. The submission to fear was never to be an option for my brother and me.

Our mother's influence was not just limited to my brother and myself. Throughout our childhood, Mom was that aunt, cousin, niece, in-law, etc. who would get on everyone, anytime and everywhere. She fussed at everyone. I recall relatives going out of their way to avoid her (humorously), especially if she was aware of what they were doing at home, in school, on the streets, or at their places of business. She would take them to task and put them in a headlock to make her point whenever necessary. No matter the person, or the place she encountered them, she would challenge everyone to recognize their God-given potential. That was her gift, and it continues to reap an endless bounty. Mom was the visionary. Our father was the hammer.

Dad, a veteran of the United States Marine Corps, and a retired United Auto Worker of America was the hammer to drive home the nail to ensure Mom's vision came to fruition. He worked very hard. My brother and I joke about Dad resembling the character, James Evans, Sr., from the 1970s television sitcom, *Good Times*. Knowing the impact of having a father who was there everyday, I dissent from the conclusion that responsible fatherhood only goes so far in a world plagued by institutionalized oppression.[2] The James Evans character symbolized all I recall seeing throughout my formative, adolescent and early adult years. Our father was flawed, an imperfect human being, who gave everything he had to make sure his family had food on the table. The bills were paid and discipline was imposed when

---

2. Smith, Michael Denzel, The dangerous myth of the "missing black father". The Washington Post, 1/10/2017.

our conduct or classroom performance fell below his expectations. Most importantly, and just like the character, James Evans, Sr., our father was there, at home, every day of our lives. We knew that, if push came to shove, he would have the last word in our home. Dad was hard and demanding. Yet, he is the father most boys dream of having. He taught us to fish, sharing his passions for sports and the outdoors. In addition, he taught us the importance of forgiveness and unconditional love when we messed up.

Our father is a very intelligent individual. He is knowledgeable about politics, economics, and history. Whenever I would tell him about what a teacher or college professor said in class, he was quick to remind me to be careful not to accept everything as truth. He would say, "Check things out for yourself. If something doesn't sound right, don't be afraid to question it." If it came down to receiving a particular grade, he would tell us to be sure to distinguish between what you know to be the truth, and what the teacher requires, especially if your final grade depends upon it. Our father was involved in our lives. He attended our sporting, and other school-related, events. We always watched sporting events and movies together. We ate dinner with him every evening. Unlike the crisis people generally associate with "black fatherhood" today, no such crisis existed in our lives. He was a hands-on father.

Although Dad was the principal disciplinarian in our household, he also understood the reality of racism and bigotry that permeated the city of Buffalo. He grew up there. He witnessed segregation and was subject to discrimination first hand. On more than one occasion, we were cautioned not to frequent certain areas of the city due to its level of hatred and hostility exhibited toward black people. Although the area in which we lived in North Buffalo provided our family with an inclusive and diverse experience, it did not mean the issues of social justice were not being championed within our household. From as young as I can remember, our parents always reminded us of who we were and how the world would react to us if we were not prepared to receive and process the hostility we would face as we got older. It was difficult to reconcile this teaching with the unconditional love we received from our "extended family." For a lot of kids, like my brother and I, "preaching" can fall on deaf ears, until the reality in which we live comes full circle and thrusts your father in the position of becoming your champion.

Where I attended high school outside the city of Buffalo, there was a large number of kids from the city who attended the school. Including myself, approximately twelve to fifteen black males also attended the school. The daily commute was a long one, requiring us to take multiple buses to reach our location. Then, we were required to walk nearly a mile from the bus stop to the school through a residential neighborhood. On an unseasonably warm spring day in 1982, we walked from the school to our designated bus stop. The bus was waiting, and we boarded. I vividly recall all of the students being riled up. Soon after boarding the bus, students began removing the paper advertisements that were posted inside the bus from their designated locations. As they were being removed, they were being torn and thrown up to the front of the bus. I recall being seated in the middle front section of the bus with another student. Ultimately, the scene on the bus resembled a party on wheels. Not too long into the trip, I saw a student pull out a blade from his coat pocket and cut the passenger cord that would be normally pulled by passengers to advise the driver their stop was coming up. The cord was pulled out from its position and discarded. Near my seat, I saw one of the advertising signs on the ground; I picked it up and ripped it and tossed it aside. Once I arrived at my stop to catch my next bus, I didn't think much of what I had done or what had transpired on the bus until the next school day when I boarded the bus to go home again.

The following afternoon, I attempted to board the bus to go home. It was at this time that the bus driver took my pass and the pass of the other student who sat next to me the previous day. He took the passes with no explanation. The next day, when I was at school, I was asked to report to the principal's office. When I arrived, my father was present and sitting at a conference table. Seated at the same table were our high school principal, the bus driver, and a representative of the bus agency, which operated the metropolitan bus system in, and around, Buffalo. Our principal asked me to take a seat. Upon doing so, I vividly recall all faces being affixed upon me intensely. I had not been made privy to the discussion that transpired before I arrived. With my father being present, I knew he had been called out of work. I can only imagine the nature of the discussion that took place between my parents that resulted in him being the one to drive to my school and attend this meeting. Thus, I knew before I was asked to explain what happened on the bus that my father expected me to tell the truth. He demanded truth above all else. He knew when most people were trying to "shuck and jive" him, and this was not the day to do it. On this day, in this instance, the truth was not only the most preferable response to give; it was the only one.

After I had taken my seat, my principal turned to me and asked, "Elvage what happened on the metro bus yesterday? Did you have anything to do with the vandalism that took place?" I told him the extent of my involvement was tearing an advertisement that had been pulled out from the frames that were positioned above the windows of the bus. My father quickly chimed in, and for the first time in my life, I watched how "Dad" instantaneously transitioned into my advocate. At fifteen years of age, this was a revelation unlike any other. Dad was not the kind of person who made it a habit of accepting an excuse from us when our conduct fell below his expectations. When we would attempt to explain something, even if it was not our fault, he would not relent. He demanded that we always acknowledge the part we played in a situation that may not be exclusively attributed to our conduct. He expected the highest degree of honor from me and Terrance. To see him passionately convey his belief in his son's position, and assert that this bus driver randomly picked me and another black student out of a bus filled with over eighty passengers who were predominantly white, showed me first-hand how important it is for me to be prepared to speak for those who don't have the ability to defend themselves. I didn't know why I was being accused of causing hundreds, if not thousands, of dollars of damage to this bus. All I recall is my father relying upon logic to surmise that I could not have caused the damage the bus driver attributed to me. My father was able to effectively demonstrate to the satisfaction of those in the room that the accuracy of the representations made by the bus driver were not reliable. The bus driver acknowledged that I and the other student had been sitting at a location that made it physically impossible for either of us to have cut the bus bell cord and vandalized other areas of the bus. There were too many points of origin for the physical damage that was committed. The extent of the damage could not be attributed to the two of us. My father passionately articulated to everyone in the room the only reason why I and my fellow student were identified out of a whole busload of high school students was because of the color of our skin. Dad showed me a side of himself I didn't know existed. It did occur to me, however, that the level and strength of his position and the depth of his analysis was not just because I am his son; it was a product of his unyielding belief in me.

Subsequent to this exchange, I was told I could return to my class. Later that same day, I was called down to the principal's office, and he discussed with me the events of the day, as well as his future expectations of me. I can only imagine he had a similar discussion with the other student. Subsequent to this meeting, my bus pass was returned to me, and my riding privileges were restored.

When I arrived home later that day, I don't recall my parents discussing the matter further. My parents reaffirmed their expectations of me and my behavior. That was a day that has forever remained with me. I knew who I could be, and how I could handle myself, even in the midst of a situation when people underestimate my strength and my ability to fight for what is right and just. Thank you, Dad.

Mom and Dad were ideal parents, good neighbors, and they cared for others. However, their marriage was a complex one. They were married nearly forty-seven years before they divorced. When my parents married, my father was twenty-four, and our mother was twenty. Our mother, a product of Batesville, Mississippi, spent her formative adolescent years in Memphis, Tennessee. She was visiting relatives in Buffalo at the time my parents met. Dad was born in Camden, South Carolina. When he was under the age of ten-years-old, his family moved to Buffalo. Both experienced the full implications of Jim Crow and the limitations it placed on people of color. They would admit that there were a lot of good times and not-so-good times during their marriage. But there was one aspect of their lives to which they were in agreement: how they wanted to raise their sons. Terrance and I were always the priority. No degree of friction between the two of them would degenerate into division that would provide my brother and me the opportunity to take advantage or play one against the other. Mom demanded that we respect and fear our father. When push came to shove and we were not listening to her, all she had to do was tell us, "I am going to let your father deal with you when he gets home." That was not what we wanted to hear. We knew what that meant. Dad was equally adamant about reminding us to do those things Mom expected of us.

Mom and Dad cultivated and maintained a family unit that provided for our most basic needs. We never lacked for shelter and protection. Both were demanding. However, their demands of us were not extreme or unreasonable. As I consider the nature of the environment in which we were raised, the most appropriate word I would use to describe it is "balance." Our childhood was filled with a balance that we were unable to appreciate at the time. When our parents began to see or hear evidence of us embracing any form of extremism, they were quick to remind us to think for ourselves and only come to a conclusion when we have all of the available information. An example of this happened one day when I returned home from school. Our mother had just prepared dinner, and we were sitting down to eat. Somehow, the discussion turned to the lack of jobs and the unemployment rate in America. It was not too long after Ronald Reagan was elected President of the United States. Earlier that day, this same subject had been discussed in one of my classes, and I repeated an assertion I heard another student make. This student attributed the rate of unemployment in the United States to the number of "foreigners" who were coming into our country and taking our jobs. I repeated this assertion in the presence of my parents at the dinner table. Almost immediately, they challenged not only the claim I was repeating but also helped me understand that I didn't have a complete understanding of the issues. Both knew that my statement was the product of a fifteen-year-old boy who needed to be enlightened. I remember my father being a great deal more forceful with his response. He raised his voice and said, "Sounds like you are repeating what you heard from those people at that school. Do you realize the jobs worked by the people who come to this country are not the jobs white Americans want to work?" I had never heard this side of the issue before. My parents understood that it was their job to make sure my brother and I understood the rules and dynamics that governed this world. Although they both believed in the importance of obtaining a good education, they didn't abdicate their responsibilities for our education and development to those whose perspectives and experiences were significantly different from their own. Our parents cautioned us to receive and study information without necessarily allowing our opinions and lives to be influenced by it. Mom and Dad kept it real. When I became an adult, I recall attending a church service and hearing my former pastor say something that made me recall these experiences and conversations with my parents. He said, "The truth is the tension between two extremes." It was a reminder to guard against the onslaught of radical opinions and beliefs and to always maintain a balanced perspective.

Mom and Dad had been subject to the cruel world of discrimination and racism. Nevertheless, they always tried to view people and the circumstances through the lenses of fairness and truth. When they missed the mark, they never made excuses. They always exhibited a willingness to acknowledge their shortcomings. But they never accepted excuses from us, no matter how well-articulated and understandable the reasons may have been. They knew all of the issues and struggles that gave rise to the anger and rage of black people. Together, they made sure we were equipped to identify and understand the inequities and injustices that exist, while being prepared to respond and address them through charitable acts of giving and service. Mom and Dad's abilities to empathize were not just relegated to people of color. They were committed to responding to the needs of all people. I can only imagine how many people our parents assisted at critical moments in their lives and effectively altered and changed their viewpoints and perspectives about black people.

I now walk in the footsteps of my parents. Mom and Dad adopted a commitment to utilize their black experiences as the engine to kick-start and internalize their attitudes that allowed them to manage their anger and pain. But, for their approach to the circumstances they faced, our parents would not have been able to help us distinguish between the hostile bias and the natural curiosity of the white people we meet, and recognize those who are in a position to assist us in the pursuit of our own endeavors.

We carry the future dreams and expectations of my parents' generation. Regardless of their motives, Mom and Dad made sure I understood that the people I would be fortunate to encounter throughout my lifetime had no obligation to bestow their advice and share their experiences with me. Once, Mom said, "They do it because they see something in you—something you don't see in yourself." Although these contacts—and in some cases, relationships with my former neighbors or acquaintances of our parents—were no doubt invaluable, they were outside of my traditional family structure. Ultimately, it was within the structure of my family where I was able to understand and appreciate the benefit of these contacts and relationships and how they might be relevant to my understanding of the world. Parents can be effective transitioning agents for their children. My parents' respective experiences, relationships, and life lessons equipped my brother and me to navigate the "issues of life" and live up to the core principles of our nation's *Preamble*.

Chapter XV

Conclusion: My Letters to America

Dear America:

Our life experiences are unique. We are often treated as strangers in the land in which we are born and raised. We encounter hostilities, disrespect, and injustices others have chosen to ignore. Life, for us, is not supposed to be easy. Yet, we continue to rise above it all. We are molded and shaped to navigate and overcome racism and bigotry. We aspire to receive a good education, have safe homes, and live in peace. And some of us seek to marry and rear children. We are committed to living in unity in order to form a more perfect union, establish justice, and insure domestic tranquility. In order to provide for the common defense, we serve in, and are represented in, the branches of our nation's military. To promote the general welfare, we continue to serve as police officers, firefighters, paramedics, doctors, and nurses. We are asked to secure the blessings of liberty for our descendants and ourselves. The Preamble and the Constitution were not drafted with us in mind. Nonetheless, it remains a debt owed to us by our country. The debt we owe is to one another.

We know the history of systemic racism and discrimination and its impact on our families and communities. This legacy must not become the legacy of our posterity. We must choose to reject the historic and oppressive conditioning that tell us we must sit by and accept the crumbs that fall from the table of others. We are capable of building a table of our own. Do not become divided over the variability of our skin tones, hair texture, or differences in wealth. Do not fall prey to the temptation to harm one another. Let your creativity, competitive desire, and ingenuity foster excellence. It is the least you can do for our posterity.

Conclusion: My Letters to America

Dear America:

I know you are not all racists. Some of you might say, "I don't have a racist bone in my body," "I have black friends," or "I don't see color." You are genuinely a nice person. You mean well. You might be a Christian. Being a good, kind-hearted Christian is not always enough. I need you to see me as I am. When you tell me you don't see color, I interpret it as you not wanting to see or acknowledge my struggle or the pain that results from my day-to-day encounter with prejudice and bigotry. I cannot separate my skin color from the experience that shapes my life's journey.

I know you have struggles and challenges. I have some of the same ones in addition to the ones that accompany my skin tone. I know it troubles you when people say, "White people benefit from privilege." The privilege of which some speak does not equate to financial wealth and problem-free living; it equates to the benefit of the doubt you receive when you walk into a grocery store, the manner in which you are greeted, apply for a mortgage, the priority you receive when you walk into a restaurant, and the level of intelligence people assign to you before you open your mouth to speak.

Every encounter for me is a moment I must be prepared to represent myself in a way that guarantees fair and just treatment that you take for granted every day. Are you followed around in a store upon entering? Have you been pulled over by a police officer for driving a nice car without committing a violation of the law? Are your peers quick to comment on your level of articulation after they have heard you speak? If the answer to each question is "no," then you, my friend, are the beneficiary of a privilege I will never know.

About the Author

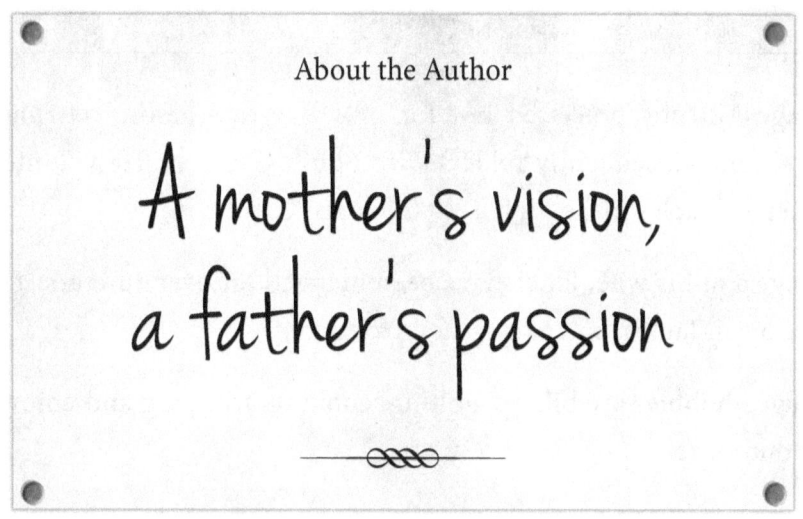

A mother's vision, a father's passion

Elvage Murphy, J.D. was born in Buffalo, NY, on August 31, 1965. His parents are Girard Murphy and Mary Murphy. He attended Buffalo Public Schools through the 8th grade, before attending Cardinal O'Hara High School, Tonawanda, New York. He attended Edinboro University of Pennsylvania. He earned a Bachelor's of Science Degree in Business Administration with a Minor in Political Science (1987) and a Bachelor's of Science Degree in Economics (1988). In 1994, he earned his Juris Doctor from the West Virginia University College of Law. Upon passing the Bar for the Commonwealth of Pennsylvania, he served as a prosecutor for the Erie County Office of District Attorney from 1995 through 2001. He served as an Assistant Public Defender for the County of Erie, before accepting a faculty position with Edinboro University where he served for over 16 years.

Elvage Murphy practiced law for over 22 years before retiring in 2015, and subsequently relocated to South Carolina. He volunteers as Lead Coach for the First Tee of Coastal Carolinas.

Elvage and his wife, Janel, have been married for over 28 years. They have a son James, and a daughter, Heléna.

Elvage's hobbies are biking, golfing, cooking, traveling and enjoying the outdoors.

www.ingramcontent.com/pod-product-compliance
Lightning Source LLC
Chambersburg PA
CBHW022017290426
44109CB00015B/1198